LINCOLN'S VANDALIA

LINCOLN'S
VANDALIA

A Pioneer Portrait

BY

WILLIAM E. BARINGER

Illustrations by
ROMAINE PROCTOR

A PUBLICATION OF
THE ABRAHAM LINCOLN ASSOCIATION
SPRINGFIELD, ILLINOIS

New Brunswick
RUTGERS UNIVERSITY PRESS
1949

CONTENTS

v

ILLUSTRATIONS

PART ONE

WILDERNESS CAPITAL

WILDERNESS CAPITAL

THIS is the story of a man and a town. The setting is Vandalia. The hero — or, as Vandalia saw him, the villain — is Abraham Lincoln. Motorists on U. S. 40 between Terre Haute and St. Louis encounter modern Vandalia as a peaceful town in central Illinois, differing from a thousand others only in a vague tradition of historic events long past. Vandalia is ancient as settlements go in this part of the world. More than a century ago the chief business of the state was centered here. But the day of its glory was brief. Here also began a career in public affairs destined to be of great and permanent importance. The development of the man and the decline of the town were closely interconnected.

If "all the world's a stage," Abraham Lincoln of Sangamon County was a prominent actor on the rustic boards of Vandalia, pioneer capital of Illinois. Tall, slightly stoop-shouldered, young yet weather-beaten, with a face long, lined, and angular, the youthful lawmaker's melancholy appearance changed surprisingly in humorous conversation as his expression brightened and his eyes sparkled, "all terminating," declared a colleague, "in an unrestrained laugh in which every one present willing or unwilling [was] compelled to take part." Acting with the *dramatis personae* of the log-cabin capital of Illinois, young Lincoln found constant opportunity to expand, to match his wits and works with the important men of the state, to enjoy himself and to enlarge his accomplishments. His colleagues and associates, typical American pioneer leaders, were men who have been largely forgotten. Seen in their contemporary setting, they are figures no less fascinating than the young giant who was destined for great fame.

From these men Lincoln learned much. Assuming his first

3

elective office in December, 1834, within a year he had established himself as a man of mark, and within two and a half
years had won a major victory which remained his outstanding
achievement for two decades. Associating with the leading
figures of the state, he, an obscure local politician, met the
"great men" on terms of equality and quickly discovered that
he could cope with, even lead, the best of them. In the muddy
village of Vandalia he learned and practiced the subtleties of
his trade under the example and tutelage of experienced politicians. Here for the first time he mingled in polite society with
men and women of wealth, culture, education; here he debated and heard discussed every phase of national and state
politics and economic theory, probing problems of slavery and
abolition, banking, states' rights, executive powers and
patronage, temperance, internal improvements, public lands,
tariff, education, capital punishment, judicial procedure,
financial panic. As a formative influence the Vandalia period,
1834–39, was of first importance in the astonishing career of
Abraham Lincoln.

If deprived of its Lincoln connection, the story of the rise and
fall of Vandalia, pioneer capital, and its legislative sessions,
would still be well worth the telling as social history. There
one can see, in microcosm, the growth and functioning of
American pioneer government and the early American town.

Abraham Lincoln of New Salem, novice lawmaker from
Sangamon County, first saw Vandalia on a late November day
in 1834. Seated uncomfortably in a jolting, crowded coach,
tired after a journey of seventy-five miles which had lasted
approximately two days and one night, Lincoln watched the
log cabins of the capital flow by as the Springfield-Vandalia
stage in which he rode rolled toward the town square. A blast
assailed his ears; the driver blew a horn to announce the
stage's arrival, and pulled his team to a stop in front of the
post office. A crowd quickly surrounded the dusty vehicle.
The onlookers assembled, not to see Lincoln arrive, or any

other legislator (for lawmakers were familiar sights to Vandalia citizens), but to inquire for mail and learn the news passengers might bring. Lincoln climbed down in the wake of a tall, elegantly dressed young man, John Todd Stuart of Springfield, who knew his way about in the capital.

The towering Lincoln, dressed in the first expensive suit he had ever owned, claimed his bag, hastily surveyed the public buildings and the more numerous taverns on the square, then followed Stuart into one of the inns, registered, and took up residence as Stuart's roommate, under the same roof with some thirty other temporary residents. Few of these knew anything about him. When first mentioned by the Vandalia paper his given name was unknown in the capital; he was listed in August as "—— Lincoln," an elected representative. But Stuart was in familiar surroundings, and, politician-like, he introduced his protégé to all comers. Those who greeted Lincoln in the hearty style typical of the times grasped a hand large, hard, and strong, and regarded a man who was strikingly tall—even among tall men—and of lean, powerful build, dark, intelligent rather than handsome of feature. Kentucky-born and Indiana-reared, of an undistinguished frontier family, the newcomer had been loosely educated, and was without advantages save those he made for himself. Vocationally he was a part-time man—law clerk, postmaster, surveyor, laborer, soldier, riverman, business man, grocery clerk—and now part-time lawmaker. Such variety of endeavor indicated neither superficiality nor extraordinary versatility, but an ambitious man of ability searching for his true career. Of excellent mind, with a strong flair for self-expression, witty, not without guile, young Lincoln had developed into an individual who was studious, serious, yet gregarious, with an inexhaustible fund of humor and good-fellowship. Such a personality, in the frontier environment of Illinois, naturally found public life the most attractive field of action.

Like many of his legislative colleagues, Lincoln was a comparatively new citizen of Illinois. Arriving early in 1830 from southern Indiana, he had turned up in New Salem on the Sangamon River in 1831, in pursuit of employment promised by a frontier commercial magnate named Denton Offutt. Offutt's enterprise lasted a year, whereupon Lincoln spent four months as a soldier in the Black Hawk War, first as captain by election, then as private. Failing to win election to the Eighth General Assembly in August, 1832, the ambitious young giant staved off unemployment by entering a merchandising partnership. The firm of Berry and Lincoln, general store, did not prosper, and Lincoln augmented his slender financial resources by frequenting, as witness and juror, courts of law in Springfield and New Salem, performing minor legal services, and accepting appointment as New Salem postmaster. This office was hardly important enough to attract any prominent Democrat, so it went to an avowed Clay man. A second small piece of Democratic patronage, appointment as deputy surveyor of Sangamon County, came his way. Sighting the chain was the young politician's chief activity when the 1834 legislative campaign season arrived, and this time he ran successfully.

Many historians of Lincoln have theorized at considerable length concerning the reasons for his political affiliations. Born and reared, in his own words, in "the most humble walks of life," he spurned the party led by the "people's hero," Andrew Jackson, then dominant both in Illinois and in Sangamon County, and joined the "aristocratic" party of Henry Clay. But young Lincoln's choice of political associates was strange in appearance only. A party of aristocracy in the frontier state of Illinois—nonsense! The Clay men of the state were fully as democratic as the Jacksonians. Voters of Illinois believed in equal rights so firmly that the theory was extended to lower animals. A law of 1836, for example, which prohibited undersized bulls from running at large and propagating inferior cattle, aroused a storm of opposition. The law was denounced as aristocratic, "intended to favor the rich." Equality of rights among bulls and their owners was vociferously demanded, and numerous politicians responsible for the "little bull law" were permanently removed from public life.[1]

Young Lincoln's political ideas, furthermore, were formed in the time of "men, not measures." The men who aroused the young Hoosier's interest in politics were not Jacksonians. Clear evidence shows that before he reached voting age Abraham had become intensely interested in politics and speaking on public affairs as an appropriate field for self-expression. Soon after his arrival in Illinois he witnessed a legislative canvass, as candidates for election to the Seventh General Assembly mounted the stump in Macon County. Hearing William L. D. Ewing and John F. Posey address the electorate in Decatur one summer day, he was moved to stand up and make a speech of his own. But he could not vote on election day, August 2, for he had not lived in the state the required six months.

Two years later he was prepared to vote and to run for the legislature. He had no intention of beginning his political career by winning a minor office and working up. Rather he would begin near the top, without benefit of the oft-mentioned proddings of Miss Ann Rutledge or Miss Mary Todd, for the legislature was paramount in the government of Illinois. Plans were made well in advance of the campaign season. Though it was the era of "men, not measures," Abraham had no powerful friends to help him along. So he appealed for votes by taking a public stand on current issues locally important. With great care he drew up a long document which he caused to be published in the *Sangamo Journal* at Springfield, March 15, 1832, declaring to all voters of Sangamon County his belief in internal improvements and public education, his opposition to loaning money at high interest rates, his desire to improve laws regarding estrays, roads, and execution of court judgments. But he spoke as an authority only on the subject of river navigation. Citing his experience as a Sangamon River boatman, he declared his conviction that the river could be made navigable by spending a moderate sum of money to clear and straighten the channel.

But, Fellow-Citizens [he wrote], I shall conclude. Considering
the great degree of modesty which should always attend youth,
it is probable I have already been more presuming than becomes
me. However, upon the subjects of which I have treated, I have
spoken as I thought. I may be wrong in regard to any or all of
them; but holding it a sound maxim, that it is better to be only
sometimes right, than at all times wrong, so soon as I discover my
opinions to be erroneous, I shall be ready to renounce them.

Every man is said to have his peculiar ambition. Whether it be
true or not, I can say for one that I have no other so great as that
of being truly esteemed of my fellow men, by rendering myself
worthy of their esteem. . . . I am young and unknown to many
of you. I was born and have ever remained in the most humble
walks of life. I have no wealthy or popular relations to recom-
mend me. My case is thrown exclusively upon the independent
voters of this county, and if elected they will have conferred a
favor upon me, for which I shall be unremitting in my labors to
compensate. But if the good people in their wisdom shall see fit
to keep me in the back ground, I have been too familiar with
disappointments to be very much chagrined.

> Your friend and fellow-citizen,
> A. LINCOLN.

Before the canvass actually began the young candidate
joined patriot and politician in taking up arms against war-
painted Indians in northern Illinois, returning home in time
to deliver a few speeches before election day, August 6. Four
members of the lower house were elected from a field of
thirteen candidates, among whom Lincoln ran eighth. The
showing was not too bad for a first race, but he would have to
advance rapidly to become one of the top four in 1834. That
such an advancement might not be impossible was hinted by
his vote in the New Salem precinct, 277 of 300 votes cast. New
Salem lay in the northern part of Sangamon County. He must
make himself equally well and favorably known in other sections of Sangamon. Just such an opportunity came in his appointment as deputy surveyor in 1833.

On April 19, 1834, Lincoln's candidacy was announced in
the *Sangamo Journal* at Springfield. John T. Stuart of Springfield had announced himself a candidate for re-election, and

the Jacksonian group of Sangamon County had put forward four opposition candidates. Lincoln did not repeat the experiment of issuing a platform. Instead, he put his faith in that bipartisan support which in 1832 had given him virtually a clean sweep in the New Salem area. During the four-month campaign he divided his time between surveying and attending political rallies. At one of these Lincoln was approached by a Democratic leader who made him a proposition: a calculated number of Democratic votes would be cast for Lincoln, with the idea of beating Stuart and electing Lincoln and three Democrats. But the surveyor-politician would make no commitments until he had talked to the prospective victim. Stuart thought himself strong enough to win anyway, so he told Lincoln to accept. Stuart's followers then concentrated on beating one of the strong Jackson candidates, Richard Quinton, giving some of their votes to less prominent Jacksonians. Quinton finished out of the money by a narrow margin. Two Whigs and two Democrats were thus elected. Lincoln ran a strong second, only fourteen votes behind John Dawson, Democrat, who led the ticket. Third and fourth places went to William Carpenter and John T. Stuart. Only Stuart and Dawson were experienced legislators, Dawson having been in the House in 1830.

For four more months the young giant from New Salem carried chain and compass; then late in November he put aside those convenient instruments of advancement and prepared to begin his career as a giver of the law. Not wishing to make his initial appearance as an elected official clad in his customary homespun, trousers failing by six inches to meet his shoes, Lincoln borrowed $200 from a New Salem friend, Coleman Smoot, and spent sixty dollars on a new suit, tailor-made in Springfield. More dollars were expended on accouterments worthy of the new position, leaving enough cash to last until he could collect his legislative salary of three dollars per day. Boarding the regular weekly stage at New Salem, he bounced slowly south to Springfield, where other Sangamon legislators came aboard. From Springfield they rode together south and east to Vandalia.

Such was the undistinguished background of the new anti-Jackson representative from Sangamon County. His political career would stand or fall by the record he made in the rough capital village, and Lincoln intently took stock of his surroundings. The community had been there but fifteen years. The tall politician, himself ten years older than the capital, was not impressed by its size. Springfield, to which he journeyed often

First House of Divine Worship
(*Erected by the State and later occupied
by the Presbyterian Church*)

on business, was much larger. But Vandalia, mecca of the politically and socially minded of Illinois, was a place of greater importance. A community of some 800 to 900 inhabitants, the capital's appearance was described in a magazine briefly published in Vandalia. "The site of the town is remarkably handsome," boasted *The Illinois Monthly Magazine.* "Around it are many beautiful elevations, which command extensive prospects. It is surrounded by timber." The country around the timber, while good, did not "contain so continuous a body of fine land as is found in many other parts of the State."

> The town is decidedly healthy. At its first settlement, it was, like all new towns, much afflicted with disease; but for the last eight years, the inhabitants have been as healthy as those of any other village in the State. . . . Excellent water is obtained in wells. . . . Wood is the only fuel used. . . . The neighboring hills abound in coal of a good quality, but none has yet been found nearer to the town than four miles.
>
> Nothing is made in this country, as yet, for export, except beef, pork, venison hams, and skins, in small quantities. . . .
>
> There are four stores for the retailing of merchandise. . . .
>
> A plain brick edifice for a State-house . . . : a banking-house, of brick, now converted into public offices; and a neat framed church, are all the public buildings.
>
> The benevolent societies of the State hold their meetings here. These are the State Bible Society, Illinois Sunday School Union, State Colonization Society, and State Temperance Society. . . .
>
> There is a school for boys, two schools for girls, and a Sunday school. . . .
>
> The national road passes through this place. It has been located from Terre Haute, in Indiana, to Vandalia; the trees have been removed from the bed of the road, and the bridges are in progress. . . . This road will be of great importance to Vandalia, as it will no doubt be the main route which will be travelled from St. Louis to the eastern States, and by the emigrants to Illinois and Missouri.[2]

Like westbound emigrants who traveled the National Road, Lincoln found that the small seat of government had taken root atop a flat bluff overlooking the Kaskaskia River. The unfinished National Road crossed the stream, led up a sharp hill, and precipitated travelers unexpectedly into the center of town, where a spacious public square was encircled by a rectangle of ramshackle buildings. Aside from two state buildings of brick, only the presence of an exceptional number of large taverns distinguished the capital from other towns of its size. Streets were simply wide spaces of mud or dust, with log cabins scattered along them. But great things were envisioned for the future, and a bevy of carpenters and allied artisans were already making inroads on the preponderance of log houses.

Residents of the capital were proud of Vandalia's history. In its founding they saw the state taking a step along the highroad of greatness. If the exploring Lincoln was not already familiar with the story of the founding of the town, he doubtless heard it before he had been there long.

A horseman had set out from the old French village of Kaskaskia on a May day in 1819. His horse carried him slowly north along the Kaskaskia River. Behind the rider, spread out on a low flat between the Mississippi and Kaskaskia rivers, lay the largest settlement and temporary capital of the new state of Illinois. The horseman was Thomas Cox, senator from Union County. He rode north on a mission which would end Kaskaskia's eminence. The old territorial capital was subject to regular floods and badly situated with respect to the state boundaries recently marked out by Congress. A stronger influence, however, in sending Senator Cox on his journey north, was desire for profit. To clear the wilderness and erect a new seat of government was expected to boost land values to the advantage of all participants. Not wishing to leave this bright prospect to chance, the politicians who made up the 1818 constitutional convention directed the first legislature to petition Congress for a grant of land farther north on the Kaskaskia River. The First General Assembly accordingly asked Congress for a grant of from one to four sections of public land for a new capital, astutely pointing out that such a course would increase the value of nearby federal lands. Congress agreed, and made a grant of four sections in March, 1819. The legislature appointed Samuel Whiteside of Madison County, Levi Compton of Edwards County, William Alexander of Monroe, Thomas Cox of Union, and Guy W. Smith of Edwards, members of the commission to locate the new seat of government.[3]

Ninian Edwards
(*Governor of Illinois, 1826–1830*)

Required by their instructions to find a site on the Kaskaskia River east of the third principal meridian (a key north-south line of the township system which bisects the state), in a region where public land sales had not yet begun, the commissioners assembled at the remote cabin of Charles Reavis, pioneer farmer. Senator Cox traveled as the river flowed not less than a hundred miles to reach the rendezvous; Guy Smith did not show up at all. Crossing the third principal meridian, the four commissioners went twenty miles up river, looking over the terrain on both banks. "After taking into view . . . the local advantages of each situation," they declared in their report to the legislature, the four examiners "did select" a picturesque wilderness highland, Reeve's Bluff (a corruption of *Reavis*),[4] fifty feet above the west bank of the river.[5] They named it, for reasons unknown, Vandalia, to be by constitutional direction capital of the state for twenty years.

Operations designed to convert the heavily-timbered headland into a thriving, prosperous city were speedily begun. But the place was twenty miles from any settlement, in a region not yet organized for county government, and progress was necessarily slow. The commissioners, charged by the legislature with the task of laying out the town after locating it, and erecting a temporary state house within six months, hired surveyors and woodsmen to drive back the wilderness. Surveyors laid out the town in August, subdividing the plot into sixty-four squares. Two central squares were allotted to public use, and each remaining square cut into eight lots. Streets eighty feet wide were laid out. A corner lot south of the reserved public squares was selected as the site of the capitol building. One Edmund Tunstall, the lowest bidder, received the building contract from the commissioners.

Town lots, announced for sale in August, were sold at public auction in September, according to legislative direction. The state government had little money in its coffers, and intended to take for itself all speculative profits. Therefore the commissioners were allowed to sell no more than 150 lots in the new stump city, and the price paid ranged from $100 to $780, a tremendous over-valuation based on grandiose expectations.[6] The average price was $234, and the state would, if all contracts were carried out, realize $35,000 from the original sale, enough to operate the state government for nearly two years. Few contracts were fulfilled, however, and the price of lots rapidly declined. On auction day a sizable crowd assembled and bidding was brisk. State officials arrived, or sent agents, to

buy lots. The surveyors invested. Everyone having a part in
the new town, except the commissioners themselves and the
state house contractor, Tunstall, paid part cash down and
gave the name of another investor as security for the remainder
of the purchase price.[7]

Log houses began to go up even before auction day. One of
the first settlers, arriving in August, encountered considerable
difficulty in penetrating the dense surrounding forest. But by
September several passable roads had been cut, and on
September 10 he wrote:

> There is already considerable activity manifested. . . . Now
> the most active preparations are being made for the construction
> of houses, and we are daily visited by travelers. But how it will
> have changed in 10 or 20 years! All these huge forests will have
> then disappeared and a flourishing city with fine buildings will
> stand in their place. A free people will then from this place rule
> itself through its representatives and watch over their freedom
> and well-being.[8]

If Vandalia could hardly claim to be "a flourishing city"
when Abraham Lincoln looked it over fifteen years later, the
last part of the prophecy at least was being fulfilled.

Among the Vandalia inhabitants who welcomed the legis-
lators at the end of November in 1834 were residents who
spoke English with a heavy accent. The young giant from San-
gamon heard them converse in their native tongue, German.
These, the first Europeans with whom Lincoln was thrown
into close contact, were the remnants of the Ernst colony.
Ferdinand Ernst, wealthy German liberal, had come to
America in 1819 seeking fertile soil for a German settlement.
Accompanied by young Frederick Hollman, "agriculturalist,"
Ernst traversed the settled portion of Illinois in wagon and on
horseback, examining the new state with perspicacious eye.
Impressed by the abundance of waterways, he found them
slow-flowing and frequently stagnant in low-water season,
productive of swarms of mosquitoes which sent settlers to bed

with fevers. Flies were the plague of horses. In summer months a swarm of huge flies might kill a horse in a short time.[9]

Ernst was impressed by the vast prairies:

> They are covered with tall or short grasses and shrubs and, indeed, no more inviting thing can be imagined for a stranger than to settle here and to live and move in this abundance of nature. He needs to do nothing more than to put the plow once into these grassy plains, . . . and his fields are splendid with the richest fruits and the most abundant harvests. How much easier is here the beginning of a planter than in the dense forest on the Ohio!

In Kaskaskia the German was astonished to hear, in a Catholic church, an eloquent sermon in French delivered by a courtly padre. Governor Shadrach Bond invited Ernst to tea "in a company of distinguished ladies." Democratic etiquette impressed the visitor. Moving north to St. Louis, Ernst was gratified to see corn growing to great heights without fertilizer in the Mississippi bottom. Reaching Vandalia while the surveyors were at work, Ernst began a log house, and rode north with a guide to look over the land on the Sangamon, praises of which he heard on every side. He found them justified. Returning to Vandalia in time for the auction, Ernst bid in four lots, made arrangements for the completion of his house, and hurried to St. Louis, Europe-bound. No steamboat was leaving for New Orleans, so Ernst bought a skiff and floated downriver, making port there a month later.[10]

Back in Vandalia, construction went forward throughout the autumn of 1819. Young Hollman, who upon arrival with Ernst had been astonished to find the capital "an unbroken wilderness" instead of a city, remained to make preparations for the colony, expected within a year. "My situation," wrote Hollman many years later, "was not enviable. Here I was alone in a country so thinly settled that it might with propriety be called a wilderness, and unable to communicate with the few persons with whom I came in contact on account of being unacquainted with the English language." But the German was better off than the American pioneers of Vandalia, who had to do their own work. Living in a pole and brush shelter, he hired "an old squatter" to erect a cabin, and explored the nearby timber, blazing trees for use in building operations.

Food production was a problem which did not arise to divert the early arrivals from building. Sufficient grain, beef, and pork was available on farms within a fifty-mile radius, and "game of all kinds . . . , bear, elk, deer, wild turkeys, wild geese, wild ducks, and fish were to be found in astonishing quantities." Most first-year Vandalians had little to do after erecting their own cabins, and Hollman found labor plentiful. He hired men to fell trees, and decided that a store was needed. Ordering a storehouse added to his cabin, Hollman went to St. Louis, bought a small stock of staples, a few cabin furnishings, and a supply of books in which he could study English through the long winter evenings. "When all was finished," he wrote, "I moved my furniture into the dwelling department and the goods into the storeroom. . . . This commenced our life of semi-civilization. Emigrants were arriving daily and building themselves primitive habitations."

In the spring of 1820 Tunstall the contractor arrived with a dozen workmen to begin erecting the state house. Slowly the building took shape. Contracted for on August 11, 1819, it was to cost less than five thousand dollars. Supposed to be ready within six months, sixteen elapsed before the government took possession. McCollum the surveyor "commenced to build a hotel and business was brisk in all departments." Hollman constructed a small brick kiln, producing brick not for houses but for cellar walls and chimneys, and contracted for three more log houses and two frame dwellings. In May he received a letter from Ernst, written three months earlier, stating that a chartered ship would presently bring a hundred Vandalia-bound colonists from Germany. Convinced that "if accommodations of some sort were not provided for members of the legislature it would be a death blow to Vandalia," he decided to erect a two-story building which might serve as a hostelry.

By summer Hollman's log houses were finished and frames of the other three buildings were standing amid stumps and weeds. Also up was the skeleton of the state house and frames of several other houses. "The place began to assume the appearance of a veritable village. Blacksmiths, shoemakers, tailors, and other mechanics were as busy as bees." [11] Autumn came and the Ernst colony did not appear. Fearful that the legislature would assemble before the newcomers could arrive, move in and prepare lodgings, Hollman furnished the houses he had built, hiring a widow Thompson from a nearby farm to make bedclothes and act as landlady at the large house.

The state house was ready in November. Late in the month state officers and legislators rode into town from day to day, expressing surprise at the dent made in the wilderness on the wooded bluff. Hollman lodged twelve legislators and boarded four clerks who slept in the state house. State papers arrived in December. Young Sidney Breese, clerk of the secretary of state, brought them from Kaskaskia in a small wagon. State officials moved in, and on December 4 the Second General Assembly convened in the barren rooms. Vandalia had become, in fact as in law, the seat of government.[12]

The legislature proceeded to incorporate the town of Vandalia, charging the town trustees to look after the state house during legislative recesses. Heated by fireplaces, the capitol was found to have chimneys which supplied the chambers with smoke as well as heat. The lawmakers authorized the town trustees to hire "some skillful person" to paint the state house and provide flues which did not operate in reverse.

The log capital, in a year and a half, had made progress. Stumps and log buildings were more numerous. Prospects in the post office were considered sufficiently attractive to arouse lively competition for the office of postmaster.[13] Population had expanded, the largest rise occurring when Ferdinand Ernst at last returned with a colony of thirty families from

Hanover. At the supper hour one evening in late December citizens were mystified by a sound never before heard in Vandalia — instrumental music. Up the steep hill leading into town from the river came a wagon conveying a band which rendered a lively patriotic air. Four more wagons contained Ferdinand Ernst and family, female and juvenile members of the colony, and household goods. A column of men marched in the rear. Hollman and his countrymen exchanged emotional greetings, and he led them to the state house where the immigrants gave three spirited cheers "for the legislature and the State of Illinois." Speedily installed in cabins and houses prepared for them, the newcomers accounted their new life auspiciously begun.

The Ernst colony contained forty-five men, thirty-five women, and some fifteen children. "Among the men were two carpenters, two blacksmiths, two butchers, and one baker. These all went to work and did well during the continuance of the legislative session." Other artisans, the building boom over, were idle. "So were most of the females. About half a dozen young girls who were both pretty and neat got good situations and most . . . grew up to womanhood and were married to American residents." The Reverend Mr. Smith, Lutheran minister, held weekly divine services in German in the state house, his audiences including Americans who understood not a word of his sermons. Ernst took over the large hotel, named it Union Hall, and operated it as a tavern and general store. Leaders of the colony were musicians of some skill, who performed in the Ernst home chamber compositions of Handel, Haydn, Beethoven, and Mozart. On weekdays Smith the preacher taught school in one of the cabins. This schoolhouse also served as the first courthouse of Fayette County. At the first meeting of the county commissioners, April 16, 1821, Ferdinand Ernst and Elijah C. Berry were named supervisors of roads. The immigrants thus quickly established themselves as "industrious and prudent citizens,

occupying their time and attention with their own business." [14]
The son of Frederick Remann, merchant, of the Ernst colony,
was to be elected to the legislature, his grandson to Congress.

Even more interesting to the visitor from New Salem than
the German inhabitants was the state capitol, hub of activity
during legislative sessions. He saw and explored a ten-year-old
brick building, plain of line and in a condition of extreme
disrepair, occupying a large lot across the street west of the
public square. This was Vandalia's second capitol; the first
had had a brief career. Occupied by the state in 1820, it had
served as the seat of government during Vandalia's infancy.

Members of the 1820 legislature, all of them non-residents,
were hard put to find lodging of any kind. Some Vandalians,
behind in payments on lots, were allowed to remain because
they had put up houses needed to accommodate the lawmakers. State officials lived in their official quarters, or main-
tained offices in their living quarters. The auditor and family
moved into this first state house, smoke notwithstanding, but
had to move out when the legislature assembled, and could
find nothing better than a tiny log cabin at the edge of the
forest. Governor Bond boarded at the residence of Robert K.
McLaughlin, treasurer, where the state treasury was also
housed, but went back to his Kaskaskia home without delay
upon adjournment.[15]

The bucolic simplicity of life in the wilderness capital of a
frontier state in 1821 can be accurately gauged by the expenditures of the first legislative session held in Vandalia. Less
than a hundred dollars was spent on stationery, including the
cost of inkstands for the new building (5 cork, 2 pewter, 1
china), bottles of ink, and quills. Writing paper cost only
$13.50. Seventy cords of firewood were burned at $1.50 per
cord. The legislature printed only 150 copies of the governor's
message, a state paper which asked for generosity in improving
the seat of government. Dignified public buildings ought to
be authorized, said Governor Bond, including a "seminary of

learning," so that the student might, "by an occasional visit at the houses of the general assembly, and the courts of justice, . . . find the best specimens of oratory the State can produce; imbibe the principles of legal science, and political knowledge, and by an intercourse with good society his habits of life would be chastened, and his manners improved." [16]

The legislature was not interested in improving the manners and chastening the habits of the younger generation. More to the point were the economic difficulties of the voting generation. The panic of 1819 had produced a severe shortage of money and made payment of debts impossible. Attempting a remedy, the legislature passed a stay-law, blocking legal judgments against debtors' property, and chartered a state bank, located at Vandalia. The capital's first brick building, the bank, began to rise on the public square in 1821. Its loose money practices made the bank popular and brought people to town. A plain building, it was not completed until September, 1822. Three months later the Third General Assembly convened. The eighteen members of the Second General Assembly who returned to the Third found Vandalia improved. Fayette County, named for the famous French marquis, had been established February 14, 1821, and several licensed taverns were seeking custom.

The Senate selected a new clerk, young Thomas Lippincott, who looked over the capital with an appraising eye. Two generations later he wrote:

> The town of Vandalia was altogether an experiment. . . . A square of reasonable dimensions . . . was retained in the center; . . . around the square the buildings needed for officers were scattered. These were temporary of course. At the . . . lower side of the square and facing it, a wooden building had been put up, two stories high—not *very* high though—sufficient to accommodate the Senate on the upper and the House of Representatives on the lower floor. . . . The style of the building was primitive and plain as a Quaker meeting house. But it answered the purposes of legislation, or most of them. . . . The furniture . . . was as plain and primitive as the

structure. No cushioned chairs, but long, hard benches were the
seats of the members. The Speaker . . . sat on an arm chair
on a platform hardly large enough to contain it, and a few inches
high, with a board before him for a desk supported by several
sticks called balusters, and a table before it for the clerk. . . .
The Senate was "like unto it," only smaller. The Governor,
Secretary of State, and other high officers who did not happen
to reside at Vandalia, had lodgings and board little if any better
than the rest. . . . It should be borne in mind that Vandalia
was only three years old at this time. . . . It had to make itself.
. . . A great state of forwardness in improvement could hardly
have been expected.[17]

When Abraham Lincoln arrived in 1834 the capital had
begun to pay the penalty of a southern location in a state that
was developing rapidly in its northern territory. But ten years
earlier the town grew slowly for the opposite reason. It was too
far north. And bad luck paid a number of calls at the struggling village in the fourth year of its history. The new bank
was severely damaged by a fire, which was quickly followed by
a bank robbery and a murder. Then the state house caught fire
in the dead of night and burned to the ground. A spring epi-
demic swept away Ferdinand Ernst and twenty more of his
colony. Leaderless and discouraged, the German clan dis-
persed. Some drifted off, while others remained to produce
descendants who still reside in Vandalia. "Business was almost
entirely prostrated," wrote one of the immigrants. "During
the sessions of the legislature . . . business was pretty good
but at all other times Vandalia was a most dull and miserable
village." [18]

The state house conflagration threatened to lead to a still
greater disaster. The legislature might, despite the law which
made Vandalia the seat of government until 1840, move the
capital elsewhere. To avert that calamity the town began to
rebuild on its own initiative. All summer in 1824 gapers
watched a new brick capitol rise near the charred site of the
old. Workmen and suppliers of materials proceeded on faith
that the state would pay them later. When the legislature met

in November they found a two-story brick building, plain and
badly constructed, ready to house the state government and
to be paid for. By the time Lincoln arrived to represent Sangamon County, the second state house was nearly ready to fall
down.[19]

Young Lincoln, already a story-teller of parts, picked up new
material as he listened to Vandalians and colleagues regale
him with the adventures, customs, and notable characters of
capital history.

Like every pioneer community, early Vandalia had its
rowdy element. Gambling was a popular pastime, especially
during legislative sessions. A citizen told the lawmakers in 1824
that a stranger "would be hardly led to suppose there was a
statute in existance [sic] here against gambling, when he sees
it publicly practiced in various forms, under your very noses." [20]
When the game of ninepins, a favorite vehicle of wager, was
placed under ban, a new game, tenpins, was quickly invented.
The town trustees, conscious of local dignity as the seat of law
and justice, prohibited brawling. Enforcement of municipal
regulations against fighting would have been difficult if not
impossible, had not the custom taken hold of settling arguments at a place called the "Bull Pen." At a pond on the
northern edge of town contestants gathered when personal
combat was imminent. Honor satisfied, the sporting event in-
variably ended at a nearby tavern.[21]

A frequent occupant of the Bull Pen was Old Tom Higgins,
celebrated Indian fighter. Only thirty-five in 1825, Higgins
was regarded as aged because he had only one ear and bore
countless scars won in warfare with the Indians of Illinois
Territory. On the streets and in the taverns the warrior had
entertained listeners by the hour with accounts of the time he
stood off a band of Indians single-handed, with four bullets in
his body and a serious tomahawk wound in the head; or his
more recent exploit in the Galena lead region, where he fought
a legal duel with rocks at ten yards, and made his opponent

run for his life. Higgins was the champion at all forms of sport
— corn shuckings, logrollings, horse races, fisticuffs. To show
his prowess he was wont to chew up the glass after tossing off
his whiskey.[22]

Politics of the 'twenties were similarly obstreperous, and
earlier campaigns furnished material for nostalgic reminiscences retailed by the somewhat tamer politicians of the
'thirties. The typical politician had been he who appeared in
the larger towns on Saturday afternoon, dressed like his constituents in homemade cottons or linens, and engaged with
each public house to supply free liquor. Women never came
near these rallies, but men poured in by every road from miles
around, tied up their mounts, and were harangued by the
candidates "from wagons, benches, old logs, or stumps newly
cut, from whence comes the phrase 'stump speeches.' "
Vigorous oratory over,

> then commenced the drinking of liquor, and long before night a
> large portion of the voters would be drunk and staggering about
> town, cursing, swearing, hallooing, yelling, huzzaing for their
> favorite candidates, throwing their arms up and around, threat-
> ening to fight, and fighting. . . . Towards evening they would
> mount their ponies, go reeling from side to side, galloping
> through town, and throwing up their caps and hats, screeching
> like so many infernal spirits.

Occasionally a drunk would fall off his horse in the wrong
place and be found dead in the mud of the river bottom.[23]

When the Seventh General Assembly met in December,
1830, the year young Lincoln arrived in the state and interested himself in Illinois politics, Vandalia reached its tenth
anniversary as the seat of government. In this period the
population of the state had tripled. Immigrants had poured
into the central region. Until about 1828 there had been doubt
as to the permanence of Vandalia. Citizens tacitly realized,
but would not admit, that the town had been "forced into
existence unsupported by the surrounding country. That the
spirited improvement which marked the commencement of

this place," wrote a citizens' committee in 1834, "should have slackened and at last wholly ceased for a time, is what the experienced might have anticipated. Since 1828, at which period the farms in our vicinity became productive, there has been a steady and healthy improvement, which has been annually increasing." Independence Day had become an occasion of unfailing public celebration. A parade was always followed by a meeting at which some local celebrity read the Declaration of Independence, and another delivered a patriotic speech, which was followed by a public feast or barbecue punctuated by toasts and discharges of firearms. Sometimes a dance on the green for the people, a ball for the gentry, concluded the festivities. Not a soul was to be seen on farms for miles around on July 4; everyone was in town celebrating.[24]

An east-west stage line ran through town, bringing mail and passengers on the old post road between Vincennes and St. Louis. Several highlights came each week when the driver was heard blowing his horn as the stage, pulled by six horses, bowled toward the square in a cloud of dust. Every citizen who possibly could, dropped whatever he or she was doing to rush to the tiny post office, peer hopefully for mail, and discuss news brought in by driver and travelers. The fare, six cents a mile and up, dictated continued use of horseback and wagon travel for most. By 1830 post roads ran "in every direction," and mails arrived by stage or postrider from east, west, and south.[25]

When James Hall of Shawneetown, elected treasurer in 1827, came to Vandalia, the reviving town acquired a pioneer man of letters. In one of the rude cabins a book was written: *The Western Souvenir, a Christmas and New Year's Gift for 1829*, edited by Hall and published in Cincinnati in covers of bright red silk. Hall organized a historical society, and in 1830 began publishing the state's first literary periodical, *The Illinois Monthly Magazine*. Hall wrote most of the contents, chiefly essays on manners and customs, articles on Indian history, sentimental stories and Byronic verse, intended to put the

American West on the literary map. An English traveler who visited Vandalia in 1830 wrote of his surprise that, in a town only a decade old, "three annual meetings of an antiquarian and historical society have already taken place, and the whole of their proceedings are as regular, as well conducted, and as well printed . . . as if the seat of the Society had been at Oxford or Cambridge." This intellectual pre-eminence was short-lived. In 1831 the magazine moved to Cincinnati, and Judge Hall followed in 1833.[26]

During the biennial sixty- to seventy-day sessions of the legislature, the wilderness capital was crowded to capacity and beyond. Simultaneously the Supreme Court was in session. Lobbyists and hangers-on appeared in large numbers. Government expenditures, once a mere fifteen to twenty thousand dollars a year, had mounted to fifty thousand annually, making lobbying worth while. And the legislature now dealt with larger projects—internal improvement schemes, incorporation of railroads and other ventures—bringing to town lobbyists interested in profits as well as in measures. The legislature itself increased, after the 1830 census, from forty-two members to eighty-one.

Many legislators, finding accommodations now available for their wives, brought them to Vandalia for the session. Arriving with trunks and portmanteaux bulging with their finest dresses, the ladies produced a social season which ran simultaneously with the legislative session and made Vandalia the social center of the state. Aristocratic ladies from the South did their best, in a continual round of balls, receptions, parties, and private theatricals, to match the magnificence of their sisters in Charleston and Mobile. Making allowances, one concludes that the social whirl was something between brilliant and Boeotian.

A lively season was at hand as the warm autumn days of late November, 1834, passed into history. Members of the legislature arrived unheralded on horseback, or by stage, with the driver's horn blowing and citizens hurrying toward the square to meet the mail. The coach from Springfield pulled to a halt in the dust on Saturday evening, November 29, at dusk, discharging a load of passengers cramped from the long ride over primitive roads. Six of them were Sangamon County legislators, two senators and four representatives. As all climbed out, onlookers saw two men of average height, John Dawson and William Carpenter, farmers and Democrats, and two of taller build who called themselves Whigs—slender, handsome John Todd Stuart, and beside him a less elegant, but taller, figure, one Abraham Lincoln.

PART TWO

ENTER LINCOLN OF SANGAMON

ENTER LINCOLN
OF SANGAMON

THE capital community to which Stuart introduced his tall colleague was an overgrown village of large ambitions. Editor James Hall, describing Vandalia in *The Illinois Monthly Magazine*, wrote extensively of the Kaskaskia River as a potential great highway of commerce.[1] Commercial pre-eminence was still a dream in 1834, despite the revival of business as the legislature prepared to go into session. The *Illinois Advocate and State Register*, Vandalia's Democratic newspaper, reported that the capital contained, in December, 1834, "fifteen wholesale and retail establishments, all doing a fair business, besides many curious manufactures." The log capital was palpably growing up. In 1833 the post office acquired a postmark stamp more imposing than that of St. Louis. Postal receipts for 1833 were $426, against $681 for Springfield. Only two other offices in the state, Galena and Jacksonville, exceeded the Vandalia figure.[2] Shortly before the legislature met, the *Illinois Advocate* declared editorially that the town had improved so rapidly as to assure its future prosperity, regardless of what the state might do about relocating the capital. Fayette County land was beginning to be appreciated, and was said to hold out greater promise to the immigrant than Sangamon or Morgan County. The editor wrote:

> In relation to the improvements of Vandalia, we shall merely mention the very large tavern house, called the Vandalia Inn, and the extensive houses of Cols. Black, Blackwell, Remann and Leidig, the dwelling house of Col. Field, and the stores of Messrs. Brown and Jordan, besides many shops, stables and out houses, together with a large Methodist Church and a smaller one for strangers — all of which are nearly completed. The Vandalia Inn

is very extensive, and every way calculated for a first rate tavern.
. . . We trust the old complaint of want of room will no longer
be heard in Vandalia.

The *Advocate* listed 34 carpenters, 3 cabinetmakers, 3 blacksmiths, 1 gunsmith, 2 bakers, 2 shoemakers, 6 "Taylors,"
1 "Waggon" maker, 3 house painters, 4 masons, 3 plasterers,
and 7 merchants, "All doing good business," 1 steam power
and 1 water power "Saw and Grist Mill." [3]

A greater interest in doing things not strictly their own business, a burgeoning cosmopolitanism, was now apparent in
Vandalia. On October 22, 1834, a "large and respectable
meeting," presided over by leading men, heard the stories,
translated from French into English, of a band of Polish exiles,
victims of the 1830 Polish revolt. Congress had offered land to
these men without a country, and some of them settled in and
near Vandalia. The new national movement to build a monu-
ment to George Washington in the city of his name called
forth a public meeting and produced a few dollars. The
venerable James Madison was national president; Governor
Duncan presided in Vandalia, with John T. Stuart as secretary. The lyceum movement, founded by Josiah Holbrook of
Boston, had reached Vandalia. Holbrook himself appeared late
in 1831 and established a "State Lyceum." Also "in a very
flourishing condition" were three state societies: colonization,
temperance, and Bible study. The Fayette County Temperance Society met habitually in the Presbyterian church "at
early candlelight." Small itinerant circuses occasionally appeared and exhibited, at high prices, an assortment of "beasts
and brutes," an art exhibition, and a few riding acts. [4]

Three years earlier James Hall had found it impossible to
conduct a book review section in *The Illinois Monthly Magazine*
because he could not obtain the new publications. But in
February, 1835, a new book store and bindery was opened by
E. Stout, offering "BOOKS and STATIONARY, consisting of *Medi-
cal*, *Historical*, *Miscellaneous*, and *School Books*." Commercial
concerns in St. Louis, Cincinnati, Philadelphia, and New York

bought advertising space in the Vandalia paper. The old *Intelligencer*, Vandalia's first newspaper, had disappeared, and the *Whig*, which absorbed it, would give up the ghost in February, 1835, leaving the *Illinois Advocate and State Register* in sole possession of the field. Published by corpulent John York Sawyer, ex-judge, aspirant for the post of public printer, the *Advocate* followed Governor Duncan's moderate Democratic politics and caused enthusiastic Jackson men to cry for a new paper in Vandalia.[5]

Business establishments waxed and waned with astonishing rapidity. Partnerships of the 'twenties, which had often changed two or three times a year, had been replaced by new ones of a less evanescent character. The firms were still general stores; specialization had made but slight progress. Foremost among the new merchants was Ebenezer Capps. London-born, a former resident of Springfield, Capps had gone to England in 1830 and persuaded a number of cousins to move to the Illinois capital. Arriving in Vandalia in the fall of 1830, aged 32, he opened a store next to the state house and speedily established himself as a leading merchant. In December, 1834, he moved into a larger building on the north side of the square, where he soon took a wife, produced a large family, and reigned as the commercial arbiter of the region. Capps' list of "prices current" was standard. He bought and sold everything, and made his name known from Chicago to New Orleans. Dour of countenance, Capps possessed native wit and independent habits which made his store a gathering place.[6]

But there were holes in the bright fabric of Vandalia's progress. Legislators not used to Spartan living cautioned wives against coming for the social season. The newspaper often failed to appear on schedule because of a press breakdown, because editor or underling was ill, or because the paper supply had run out. Mail service was frequently irregular, especially from the east. The Kaskaskia bottom, impassable at spring high water, remained nearly so until it dried out, which generally took half the summer. Grading operations across the

bottom were regularly ruined by high water. The best time for
travel was autumn, and winter before snowfall. The legislative
season of 1834–35 encountered exceptionally mild weather; no
snow fell until the end of January. Work on the National Road
between Vandalia and Terre Haute crept forward, in good
weather, at a snail's pace. Good schools had been developed,
but they were private and expensive.[7]

Charter's Tavern

The half dozen boarding taverns to be seen around the
square, lodging thirty to forty each, were not necessary to
house the legislature, there being fifty-five representatives and
twenty-six senators. But the Vandalia Inn, the National Hotel,
Charter's Tavern, the Sign of the Green Tree, and the New
White House gained the bulk of their custom from lawyers,
litigants, office-seekers, lobbyists, and devotees of social di-
version which could be found, if anywhere in Illinois, at the
center of government. Every hotel claimed possession of an
ample supply of "choice liquors" and wines. Partaking of these
delights, as a visiting reporter from Beardstown discovered,

was an invading and continually growing army of office-seekers. Why so many, he asked? Because public office offered more pay for less work, it seemed to him, than any other kind of employment. The legislature ought to cut all salaries. Despite the recent building boom, he found Vandalia,

> . . . crowded to excess. . . . The number of applications for door-keeper and clerks of the different Houses is truly astonishing. It is said there were more than eighty applicants. . . . Almost every county furnished one candidate and some several, and all urge their claims with a pertinacity altogether invincible. One founds his claims on his revolutionary services; another on services in the last war; a third shows his wounds; and tells of his exploits and escapes; a fourth was an old ranger; the next, one of the oldest settlers; another can carry a bigger log, and make a better fire than any other man; whilst another insists that he can take up the ashes better, sweep the room cleaner, and bring better water than any other living Sucker.[8]

Another observer noted the prevalence of military titles:

> The male population was made up almost exclusively of gentlemen of a military turn of mind. And the rank to which all seemed to aspire and attain was that of Colonel. If there was a Major in town I failed to make his acquaintance. We had two Captains, — Captain Eccles and Captain Linn, but . . . Captain Linn was a steamboat captain . . . and not, therefore, subject to "the articles of war," as was the balance of the gentlemen in town.[9]

The resident Colonels and visiting dignitaries of assorted rank, whenever business did not press, filled the taprooms for discussion, politics, stories, games, songs, segars, and drink. Strong drink and strong language were always much in evidence, two habits in which Abraham Lincoln reputedly did not indulge. But young Lincoln "was always as cheerful" as if he did. Southerners transplanted to Illinois, warmed by liquid refreshment, made the nights loud with plantation songs. Someone would bellow the hundred verses, and fill out the evening with new ones, of a famous Tennessee corn shucking song, "with a score or more honorable members to troll the responsive refrain, . . ."

As I went down to Shinbone Alley,
   CHORUS. *A-Hoozen John, a-Hooza;*
As I went down to Shinbone Alley,
   CHORUS. *Long time ago,*
'Twas there I met little Johnny Gladdon, etc.

Revelry sometimes became so obstreperous that the county commissioners threatened suspension of license for "having permitted disorder, riotings and drunkenness." But disciplinary action was difficult, for the taverns commanded the best of legal talent. Gaming and gambling had increased to a point requiring the county commissioners to erect, in the fall of 1833, a new and commodious "jailhouse," complete with iron bars, "dungeon room," debtors' room, and two jailers' rooms equipped with fireplaces.[10]

As Lincoln and other new legislators quickly discovered when the Ninth General Assembly convened, the nature of their lawmaking labors was primarily determined by the general condition of the state. Illinois attained the age of sixteen years on the third day of December, 1834, two days after the session began. Like a promising young man of that age, Illinois was large, strong, and unfinished. Already the state had a recorded history extending more than a century into the past, but it was a story of individuals — Jesuit priests, French traders, soldiers of kings, scattered bands of Indians, tough pioneer hunters, transplanted French peasant farmers, rivermen half-Indian, half-French — rather than of solid institutional development, material for the romancer rather than the historian.

Sixteen years of statehood had likewise failed to produce any striking manifestations of progress. The northern third of the commonwealth lay beyond the frontier line. The Indians had been swept across the Mississippi, but in 1832 they had returned and caused a war of re-expulsion. Chicago, located on the site of an ancient aboriginal community on Lake Michigan, was a log house hamlet. Profiting by great expectations founded on congressional support of harbor improvements and a canal connecting the lake with the Illinois River, the future metropolis was just beginning its sensational growth. The canal was still a dream, but lake traffic had commenced.

The population of the state, forty-five thousand in 1818, had passed two hundred thousand by 1834, the newcomers being mostly frontier farmers. Agriculture formed the economic mainstay, for trade was almost entirely local and commerce but little developed. Settlement was strung out and meandering, following lines of river and stream, with the great Illinois prairie remaining as yet unbroken.

Government continued to be carried on under the 1818 constitution, an instrument the few thousand voters of the state had never been called upon to ratify or reject. The new state of Michigan, admitted in 1836, provided for a state university at the first meeting of its legislature. Arkansas, also admitted in '36, made its first legislature notable when the Speaker of the House killed a member with his bowie knife in the House chamber. The Illinois legislature did not establish a state university until after John Wilkes Booth had terminated Lincoln's career, but neither was any member murdered during its First General Assembly. According to Thomas Ford, governor from 1842 to 1846, who dipped his historical quill in acid ink and wielded it with wit, the weight of ignorance lay heavily on the state. Early legislatures had pared down the governor's powers and increased their own. Governors were never re-elected; indeed, they found it nearly impossible to obtain any public office whatever after presiding over the state for four years. Ford wrote:

> A session of the legislature was like a great fire in the boundless prairies of the state; it consumed everything. . . . Until the new revision in 1827, all the standard laws were regularly changed and altered every two years. . . . For a long time the rage for amending and altering was so great, that it was said to be a good thing that the Holy Scriptures did not have to come before the legislature; for that body would be certain to alter and amend

them, so that no one could tell what was or was not the word of God, any more than could be told what was or was not the law of the state.

Selection of the representatives of the people, he added, was frequently motivated by "the vulgar notion that any bellowing fellow, with a profusion of flowery bombast, is a 'smart man,' a man of talents, fit to make laws, govern the country, and originate its policy." [11] The techniques of politics were adolescent. During the eighteen-twenties,

> There were no parties of Whig and Democrat, Federalist and Republican. The contests were mostly personal, and for men. As for principles and measures, . . . there were none to contend for. Every election turned upon the fitness and unfitness, the good and bad qualities of the candidates. The only mode of electioneering . . . then known, was to praise one set of men, and blacken the characters of the other.

This nonpartisanism, gratifying though it may be to chronic critics of "party politics," was productive of irresponsible and inefficient government. Citizens were unable to assign credit for good measures or blame for bad, since responsibility could not be fixed clearly upon any group of public officials. Governor Ford continues:

> During this period neither the people nor their public servants ever dreamed that government might be made the instrument to accomplish a higher destiny for the people. . . . Government was supposed to be necessary, . . . but [the people] did not want government to touch them too closely, or in too many places: they were determined upon the preservation and enjoyment of their liberties. . . . The people were, most of them, pioneers and adventurers. . . . Such persons cared but little for matters of government, except when stirred up by their demagogues. . . . The politicians took advantage of this lethargic state of indifference of the people to advance their own projects, to get offices and special favors from the legislature, which were all they busied their heads about. . . . Offices and jobs were created, and special laws of all kinds for individual, not general benefit, were passed, and these good things were divided out by bargains, intrigues, and log-rolling combinations, and were mostly obtained by fraud, deceit, and tact.[12]

Furthermore, the notion was current in New England that a fifth-rate Boston lawyer could move to Illinois and speedily become a judge or member of Congress.[13]

By 1830 the trappings of civilization were palpably encroaching upon frontier customs. The dangle-tailed coonskin cap was giving way to the hat, fringed hunting shirts to cloth coats, deerskin moccasins to shoes, homespun cotton and woolen frocks to gowns of silk and calico. The appearance of political parties was one of these manifestations of advancement. Parties would have appeared sooner or later, but their arrival was speeded by the presidency of Andrew Jackson. Old Hickory's popularity and vigorous politics influenced political practices in ways too numerous to mention. Most important, in Illinois, was the appearance of a band of Jackson adherents among the state's active politicians. They became the Jackson party, or Democrats. Their opponents became anti-Jackson or Clay men, later Whigs.[14] Jackson's great national popularity was reflected in the predominance of his followers in Illinois. But there were varieties of Jacksonians— "whole-hog" Jackson men, and coat-tail riders who let go and rode with Clay at appropriate times, contemptuously dubbed "milk-and-cider" Democrats.

Albeit after parties arrived voters were supposed to be voting for measures and not men, personality continued to count heavily, as it does today, although in lesser degree. Legislative conduct of the eighteen-thirties makes the student wonder if these new parties were not, except on election day, largely theoretical. Members of the General Assembly were not given party labels in the official *Journal* of House and Senate, or in newspaper reports, and their votes on bills did not generally follow any ascertainable party line. "Bargains, intrigues, and log-rolling combinations" might bring to passage any minority member's bill and send down to defeat the measure of any majority representative or senator.

Cynosure of attention of new members like Lincoln was the capitol on the west side of the public square, a two-story brick

structure which had been there ten years. But it looked much
older, bearing the marks of dilapidation rather than antiquity.
Falling plaster frequently punctuated the eloquence of earnest
debate. Recently the capitol had been improved by a new fence
built around the lot, and both House and Senate chambers
had been enlarged by eliminating a central hall and stairway,
knocking out walls and substituting pillars for supports. A new
stairway had been built on the south end of the building.
Lincoln of Sangamon, stepping through the front door to ex-
amine the scene of his new work, found himself in a large,
barren room covering the whole first floor. Upstairs at the
south end was the Senate chamber, at the north end a few
small offices occupied by state functionaries who complained
that their quarters, remote from the stairs, were firetraps.
Entering the House chamber, the tall, slightly stooping new
member discovered the workroom of the powerful House of
Representatives to be as unostentatiously furnished as the
common room of any tavern. Members sat at long tables,
three to a table, in movable chairs, some of which were comfortable Windsors. The Speaker sat at a similar table, slightly
elevated, equipped with a pewter inkstand. The members'
tables bore inkstands of cork. Several sand boxes were distributed about the floor, for the accommodation of tobacco
chewers and for blotting the ink on written papers—inelegant
combination, but quite in character. These men were used to
such things. Heat was provided by a fireplace and a stove,
artificial light by candles, and finally there was a water pail
and three tin cups.[15]

Here, and elsewhere around the square, the fledgling Ly-
curgus from Sangamon County watched the great men of the
state talking, smoking, drinking, entertaining, gambling, wad-
ing the snow and mud of the streets, slipping on the ice. He
saw for the first time a handsome, squat young man who
signed himself Stephen A. Douglass.[16] Young as was the
twenty-five-year-old Lincoln, this schoolteacher and lawyer
from Winchester, Morgan County, was four years his junior.

Stephen A. Douglass

Douglass was not a member of the legislature, but expected one day to be, and was in Vandalia to lobby in his own behalf as aspirant to the office of state's attorney of the first judicial circuit.

The greatest man of the moment was Joseph Duncan, governor-elect, recently the sole Illinois representative in Congress, farmer, Kentuckian, major military hero of the War of 1812 and holder of high rank in the Illinois militia. A large man, genial, modest, curly-haired, with a pug-nosed Scotch-Irish countenance, whose wife, a beautiful young heiress, had married him on the recommendation of Henry Clay, Duncan's public career was to lapse at the conclusion of his term.

William Lee Davidson Ewing, acting governor, Kentuckian, lawyer, Black Hawk War hero, was a figure of great popularity. Short, heavy, auburn-haired, his ability and generosity were admitted by all.[17] Ewing's career began in 1826 in the humble capacity of clerk of the House. Elected representative in 1830, he was made Speaker, advanced to the Senate, became United States Senator for two years in 1835, and then began to retrace his steps. Back in the House in 1838 and '40, he was elected Speaker over his competitor, Abraham Lincoln; in the next General Assembly he was again clerk of the House, but was spared the ignominy of ending where he began by his election in 1843 as auditor, in which office he was to die.

On the Supreme Court of Illinois sat the stormy petrel of Illinois politics, Theophilus Washington Smith, better known as "Tammany" Smith. New York born, he had left the United States Navy to study law in the office of Aaron Burr, and emigrated to Illinois Territory in 1816. Entering politics, he sought the attorney generalship, lost, was elected to the Senate in 1822, and in 1825, despite a hulking, undignified, entirely unjudicial appearance and bearing, became associate justice of the Supreme Court, in which capacity he acquired the reputation of never permitting the law to interfere with politics. Smith on one occasion became so angry at Governor Ninian Edwards that he confronted the great man with a pointed pistol. Edwards instantly seized the gun and swung it violently into Smith's jaw, cracking the bone and leaving him scarred for life.[18] Impeached in 1832 for "oppressive conduct" and corruption, his trial in the House, resulting in acquittal, was the most sensational legislative trial in Illinois history. It lasted a month; one of the speeches for the prosecution went on for three days.

Two more state officials were men of mark. Alexander Pope Field, perennial secretary of state, Kentuckian of aristocratic family, tall, long-nosed, of wry expression, fond of dissipation, brilliant in speech and conversation, raconteur and ballad singer, had been a member of the House for three terms before becoming secretary of state in 1828. The most eminent criminal and damage lawyer in the state, Field was out of town on a case more often than not, for he never allowed official duties to interfere with his law practice.[19] A milk-and-cider Jacksonian, Field, like Duncan, drifted into the Whig camp, and became the object of removal proceedings begun by a new Democratic governor, Thomas Carlin. Ousted at last in 1840 to make way for Stephen A. Douglass, Field was to quit the state and become secretary of Wisconsin Territory by appointment of President Harrison. The last act of his public career was destined to be the most dramatic. Removing to New Orleans shortly before the Civil War, he was elected to the House of Representatives from Louisiana when Lincoln attempted to reconstruct the state, but was refused his seat in Congress by Radical Republicans.

John Dement, smaller even than young Douglass in stature, treasurer, Tennesseean, Black Hawk War hero, began his career as sheriff, advanced to the House in 1828, and was chosen treasurer by his colleagues in 1831. He was to resign and return to the House in 1836 to fight Springfield's attempt to capture the capital, then move to northern Illinois and engage in manufacturing. Dement's career tapered off in slow time; he achieved the remarkable record of membership in three constitutional conventions, 1847, 1862, and 1869–70.

Among the twenty-six senators there were, besides Ewing, only a half dozen men of prominence, of whom three were notables. Cyrus Edwards, brother of the late Ninian Edwards, was a Marylander, retired lawyer, merchant, Black Hawk War hero, and former representative from Madison County. A Whig, Edwards was to be candidate for governor in 1838, and would return to the House in 1860 as a Republican.

George Forquer, Pennsylvanian, senator from Sangamon, former representative from Monroe, secretary of state, attorney general, and candidate for Congress, was born to poverty but rose by acting as carpenter, land speculator, lawyer, and merchant. Celebrated as an orator and writer, Forquer was also known as a man of impecuniosity no matter what position he held.

Another Democratic Pennsylvanian was Adam W. Snyder, born in poverty, a wool-curler who promoted himself to the law, and reached the Senate in 1830. A Black Hawk War veteran, a spirited speaker, of fiery, impetuous temperament, he was defeated for Congress in 1834 by Governor John Reynolds. Snyder was to defeat Reynolds in '36 and to lose to him again in the next campaign. Returning to the Illinois Senate in 1840, Snyder was to be robbed of victory as Democratic candidate for governor in 1842 by an untimely demise.

Among the crowd assembling in Vandalia's taverns were young men not yet legislators, who were destined to play large rôles in the history of Lincoln. Ninian Wirt Edwards, Whig, son of Governor Edwards, nephew of Cyrus, was on hand seeking election as attorney general of the state. He was successful, but resigned almost at once. Elected to the House in '36 and '38, to the Senate in '44, to the House again in '48 and '50, this polished, cultured aristocrat became Lincoln's brother-in-law and the social leader of Springfield. Turning Democrat, Edwards became the first Illinois superintendent of public instruction in 1854, and in his declining years wrote a dull biography of his father.

Orville Hickman Browning, another young Kentucky aristocrat, a Whig, and a lawyer, was destined to play an equally large rôle in the career of Lincoln in a national setting. Classically educated, an effective orator, a figure as dignified and courtly as though he had stepped from the pages of Henry Fielding, Browning had his fortune to make and had set about it in Quincy, where he lived in a log cabin. In the Black Hawk War he had served for a time in the same company with Lincoln. Now a candidate for the office of state's attorney of the fifth district, he was to find, on February 10, 1835, the legislature overwhelmingly in favor of another man. Two years later he would return to Vandalia a senator, become a member of the House in 1842, aspire to Congress the next year and lose to Douglass, and lose again in 1850 and '52 to another Democrat. His greatest energies aroused later by the Republican movement, he became a leader, supporting (with inner misgivings) the candidacy of Lincoln, and succeeding the late Stephen A. Douglas as United States Senator in 1861. In the Senate he became the President's spokesman, confidant, and adviser during the first year of war, President Johnson's Secretary of the Interior in 1866, and finally a member of the Illinois constitutional convention of 1869–70.

At a General Assembly of the State of Illinois, begun and held in pursuance of the Constitution, at Vandalia, on Monday the 1st day of December, in the year of our Lord one thousand eight hundred and thirty-four, the following members appeared, were qualified and took their seats, viz:

From the county of Alexander — WILSON ABLE.
From the county of Union — JOHN DOUGHERTY.
From the county of Johnson — JOHN OLIVER.
From the county of Pope — CHARLES DUNN.
From the county of Gallatin — STEPHEN R. ROWAN and JAMES HAMPTON.

. . . .

From the county of Sangamon — JOHN DAWSON, JOHN T. STUART, WILLIAM CARPENTER and ABRAHAM LINCOLN.[20]

. . . .

Most counties had one member, several had two, a few three, and two, Sangamon and Morgan, had four. Northern counties were represented by a fraction of a man. Fulton, Knox, and Henry each boasted a third of a representative, while Peoria, Jo Daviess, Putnam, La Salle, Cook, and Rock Island each possessed one-sixth of John Hamlin.

As the session opened, members strolled in, talking with colleagues and drawing lots for seats. Dressed in long, black, wide-lapelled coats, tight trousers, stiff white shirts with collars held high by neckpieces called stocks which encircled the neck with several layers of black cloth, the honorable representatives looked more dignified and formal than they were in fact. A few years earlier silk shirts with frills could have been seen, but now a few lapel embellishments of black satin or velvet were as far as the people's representatives thought it advisable to go. Veteran legislators jocularly speculated on the prospect of having to eat, this session, seven wild game dinners each week. They hoped tavern keepers could manage a meal of more civilized fare at least once or twice a fortnight.

Gazing about at his colleagues, Lincoln saw old William McHenry, patriarch of the legislature, a living personification of the state's history, complaining to listeners that Illinois was not what it used to be. An Indian fighter in two wars, pioneer who in territorial days had killed a bear with a knife in the wilds of White County, itinerant preacher and mill owner, Major McHenry was the only surviving member of the 1818 constitutional convention and the First General Assembly still in politics, and the only former senator in the House. Elected as representative from White County for the fourth time, he was to die before the end of the session.

Other celebrities of the House who drew attention were Semple, Stuart, and Cloud. James Semple, Kentuckian, Black Hawk War brigadier general, ex-tanner, lawyer, belied his humble origin by his distinguished appearance. Very tall, wearing whiskers in the style of the European aristocracy, Semple was a man of presence. Entering the House from Madison County in 1832, he was to be elected Speaker in 1834 and '36, and a year later chosen United States minister to New Granada. Returning from South America in 1842, he was to sit on the supreme bench of the state until elected the next year to the United States Senate. Fed up with politics, he would upon expiration of his term retire and devote his declining years to writing a history of Mexico, never published, tinkering with unsuccessful inventions, and building a handsome estate and a substantial fortune.

Semple made his way into the aristocracy; John Todd Stuart was born there. Possessor of the best classical education obtainable in Kentucky, young Stuart read law for two years, then moved to Springfield in 1828. Entering politics as a Clay man, he won election to the House in 1832 and now had returned with a satellite, a new member from New Salem two years his junior. He circulated through the crowd, introducing Lincoln to members whom the new man had not already met, conversing about the political climate, recalling outstanding events of the previous session. Stuart was to run for Congress two years later, lose, then win in '38 and '40. Stopped in mid-career by the subsequent Whig decline in Illinois, he was to enter the Illinois Senate in 1849. Stuart's last phase would bring him into open opposition to a former pupil grown great. Defeated as candidate for governor on the Bell-Everett ticket in 1860, he was to be elected to Congress in 1862 as a Democrat, and to lose in 1864 at the hands of another satellite, Shelby Moore Cullom.

Newton Cloud, from Morgan County, an easygoing North Carolinian, farmer, Methodist preacher, and Democrat, had been in the House in 1830 and had now returned to embark on a career of legislative service destined to total eighteen years over a forty-year period, and to include a term as Speaker, a term as senator, and the presidency of the 1847 constitutional convention.

Among the honorable members of the House who moved about meeting their colleagues were young politicians now remembered only because of their association with the tall young man from New Salem. John D. Whiteside, Democrat, representative from Monroe County, the only member of the legislature born in Illinois, was one of the famous Whiteside family of Indian fighters, hence familiarly called "General." The general had already served two terms in the House, was to advance to the Senate in 1836, and to become treasurer a year later. But none of these things would leave a discernible footprint in the sands of time. That came in 1842, when Whiteside, on behalf of James Shields, delivered to Abraham Lincoln a summons to the field of honor.

Jesse Kilgore Dubois, red-haired Whig, representative from Lawrence County, Hoosier, son of a Canadian who was a personal friend of General William Henry Harrison, boasted an incomplete college education. He was to win re-election in '36, '38, and '42, to become a merchant during lean political years, to re-enter politics as a Republican and be elected auditor in 1856, in which position he became one of that inner circle of Illinois politicians who made Lincoln the party's candidate for president.

Orlando Bell Ficklin, independent representative from Wabash County, Kentuckian, and lawyer, was to make an impression in history by persistently opposing the destiny of his New Salem colleague. At the end of the session Ficklin was elected state's attorney for his district, resigned his seat, moved to Coles County in 1837, returning to the House a confirmed Democrat in '38 and '42. Advancing the next year to Congress, he was twice re-elected, finding throughout his third term his old Vandalia colleague sitting on the opposite side of the House chamber on Capitol Hill. Returning to Congress in 1851, Ficklin bobbed up again in 1858 as a prominent supporter of Douglas, a line he followed when Douglas ran for president. Ficklin wound up his career, astonishingly, back in the Illinois House of Representatives in 1878.

To become a man of mark in this assemblage was not as difficult as might be thought. The turnover of members was rapid. Many representatives were plain men who, after one term, ran for re-election, were defeated, and lost interest completely. Serious politicians, after a similar period, hankered for a seat in the Senate or in Congress. The House in 1834 contained thirty-five first-term members besides Lincoln, seventeen second-termers, one third-term member, and one veteran of three previous terms, William McHenry. A Boston traveler, comparing Illinois with the rest of the country, found "as fair a proportion of talent in Illinois, as in any other state . . . in proportion to its population. There are, it is true, but a very few minds of the highest order . . . , but there is an unusual amount of very respectable, clever talent." [21]

Members settled themselves at ten o'clock and the session got under way. Temporary officers were appointed, and the House proceeded to elect permanent replacements. A roll call for Speaker gave James Semple of Madison thirty votes, Charles Dunn of Pope twenty-five. Lincoln and Stuart voted for the minority candidate, a less than whole-hog Jacksonian. This thirty to twenty-five division gives as good an indication as exists of the relative strength of Jackson and anti-Jackson parties.[22] As a guide to legislative action, the ratio is about as accurate as were fifteenth-century maps in guiding explorers to the New World. Though Stuart was the Whig floor leader, there was no point in putting him up, for the reliable Clay men numbered a mere seventeen. The Whig strategy was to gain favor among the milder Democrats, whose support would help Whig measures become law.

Minor officials were then selected, seven ballots being required to choose the doorkeeper. A trifling amount of business was dispatched and the House adjourned early. Tuesday morning at ten the House met, dealt with routine matters, and adjourned to reassemble at noon and hear a message from the acting governor. The remarks of W. L. D. Ewing, chief of the state for fifteen days because both Governor Reynolds and Lieutenant Governor Zadoc Casey had resigned to serve in Congress, were a mixture of rhapsody and woe. Ewing said he was sorry to be governor. Sitting quietly in chairs, the long tables occupied by arms, feet, papers, Lincoln and his new colleagues were shown a beautiful vision.

Blessed with a salubrity of climate unsurpassed, and a fertility
of soil unequaled, in the whole Valley of the Mississippi [de-
clared the acting governor], our State is progressing with won-
derful rapidity, to a most elevated station among her Western
Sisters. . . . Emigration from every state in this great and
patriotic republic, is seeking its way in thousands and tens of
thousands to this fair Delta of the magnificent valley. With the
exception of an occasional village of provincial French, but
yesterday it was an unbroken wilderness, — a trackless waste of
prairie and unsubdued forest. The beautiful rivers that wash its
borders, rolled their deep tides to the ocean unknown and unad-
mired. This "desert now blooms as the rose." It is the "*ultima
thule*" of the emigrant's hopes and aspirations. Her rivers are
the channels of her rich commerce, and the admiration of the
world. The magic wand of enterprise, industry and talent, is
working its wonders in the land. The Indian's wigwam has disappeared in the presence of the rich man's mansion, and the
poor man's cottage. Our rich prairies are converting into luxuri-
ant fields and pastures; and all the attendant blessings and advantages of christian civilization are ours, or to be enjoyed at our
bidding. Wise legislation alone can secure the consummation of
these blessings and advantages.

This Utopia needed a revised criminal code, fiscal measures
productive of greater revenue, a state bank "founded not upon
the baseless impalpable fabric of a vision — but upon a solid
gold and silver reality," better schools at both lower and
higher educational levels, a new state capitol, and transportation improvements in the form of canals or railroads or both.
Routine business proceeded as members of the Senate
walked in for the official function of examining votes for
governor and lieutenant governor in the 1834 election. Nobody
was surprised to hear that Joseph Duncan and Alexander M.
Jenkins had been elected. The next day, Wednesday, the
senators returned and took seats in the House to inaugurate
the new officials. The remarks of the governor, a Jacksonian
now in mid-career of backsliding, were confined to three
subjects: education, internal improvements, and a state bank.
He urged broad educational legislation, canals rather than
railroads, and neither favored nor disfavored a state bank.

Compared to the address of Ewing, who now sat with the senators, the new governor's remarks made dull listening. The novice legislator, Lincoln, having heard two gubernatorial messages in as many days, must have been impressed by the problems therein discussed. He had thought about them, and publicly declared his position on some of them. But the introduction of bills dealing with those issues was farthest from his thoughts. The few laws he expected to have passed at this session dealt with minuscule matters.

The session began to move forward as members gave formal notice of intention to introduce sundry bills, or offered resolutions, in the discussion of which Lincoln's voice was not heard. Rules were adopted on Thursday morning, and the Speaker made assignments to the eleven standing committees of the House. Some members were assigned to three committees; Stuart of Sangamon was placed on two. Lincoln of Sangamon was put on one committee, Public Accounts and Expenditures, which was the tenth committee in the list of eleven.

Legislation did not follow the modern method, with a hopper for the reception of bills and automatic assignment to a committee where they would die or, in due time, emerge. As expediters of legislation, committees were then less important than the two houses themselves. To start a bill, a member gave formal notice of his intention to introduce it, and two days must elapse before he could do so, an action performed on the floor of the House. Upon introduction, each bill was normally read in full by the clerk and ordered to a second reading. But members might move assignment to a committee instead, or move to lay it on the table, or move to amend. Voting was done rapidly, by voice, unless two members called for the Yeas and Nays, whereupon the roll was called and members put on record. First and second readings could not be held on the same day unless rules were suspended. Such suspension was frequently moved, but nearly always rejected until late in the session, when suspension occurred regularly. After second reading, if no adverse motion got in its way, a bill was "engrossed" and ordered to a third reading. Again time must elapse before the bill was read again and passed or defeated. Since reference to committee occurred only on occasion of a carried motion to refer, a great many bills were passed without any sort of committee action (except for technical consideration given by the final committee on enrolled bills), a procedure which underlines the simplicity of the legislative process in that day.

Committee work was generally dispatched in the evening. House and Senate chambers were too large and open for committee meetings; private lodgings and offices were best. By custom, the House chamber was regularly used after dark by the lobby, unofficial "third house of the legislature." The lobby had a perennial, unofficial president, James W. Whitney of Pike County, an eccentric, witty lawyer without a practice, part-time schoolteacher and minor official. Every legislative session brought Whitney to the capital, dressed virtually in rags, to conduct the lobby. His performances were standard sessional entertainment. Nicknamed "Lord Coke," by which distinguished cognomen he was known to everyone, Whitney opened the "third house" with remarks bearing a satirical resemblance to official messages. Matters before the legislature were discussed in speeches full of jokes and humorous allusions, and every hit produced cheers and loud laughter. "Lord Coke" permitted anyone to speak. If a speaker was not entertaining, Whitney adjourned the "house" until the bore sat down, then reconvened it for the next performer.[23] As entertainment the lobby eclipsed, on its best evenings, "farobanks, roulettes, and coffee rooms, . . . leaving them a long way in the back ground." [24]

On Friday morning, December 5, while the House considered numerous unimportant resolutions and a financial report from the auditor, Lincoln scraped back his chair, stood up, addressed himself in his high voice to "Mr. Speaker," and gave notice of his intention to introduce his first bill, "An act to limit the jurisdiction of Justices of the Peace." His notice was shrewdly timed, coming shortly after the House had rejected another member's resolution contemplating expansion of powers of the local justices.

The second week opened with a profusion of bills. One member after another introduced his, heard it read and ordered to a second reading. Lincoln's was so treated on Tuesday, while on Monday he was assigned to his first special committee. With two others, Lincoln was to study and report a measure to increase the number of election precincts in Morgan County, adjacent to Sangamon. The committee acted with such speed that in less than a day the measure was amended, reported, and ordered to third reading. An hour later Lincoln gave notice of intention to introduce his second bill. "Mr. Speaker," he said, on obtaining the floor, "I now give notice that on Thursday next, or some day thereafter I shall ask leave to introduce a bill entitled 'an act to authorize Samuel Musick, to build a toll bridge across Salt Creek in Sangamon County.' " [25]

On his tenth day as a maker of law, Lincoln considered that he had learned his way about well enough to propose a revision of the House rules: "It shall not be in order, to offer amendments to any bill, after its third reading." [26] The motion was speedily disposed of by rejection. Behind this proposal one can see the young Lincoln carefully studying House rules in his tavern room at night, wrinkling his brow as he meditates possible improvements. Thinking he has found one, he daringly introduces it, hoping to make himself a man of mark. At first glance his suggestion seems a good one, but more experienced lawmakers knew better. The absence of such a rule was not an oversight but necessity. Not having experienced the closing days of a session, Lincoln did not know about the numerous last-minute changes required in bills already passed to make them harmonize with Senate action. His intention was clearly to speed up bills and make delaying obstructionism more difficult, but the new rule, had it been adopted, would have produced the opposite result. Bills by the dozen would have died because they were not identical with the same bills as passed by the Senate.

Lincoln's Justices of the Peace bill likewise ran into difficulties. Instead of obtaining a third reading it was referred to a special committee, emerged with amendments, then was assigned to a second special committee. As the session entered its third week Lincoln introduced his bill, "An act to authorize Samuel Musick, to build a toll bridge across Salt Creek in Sangamon County," heard it read and ordered to a second reading. That hurdle was negotiated Tuesday afternoon and a third reading ordered. Upon its being so read, Carpenter of Sangamon, Democrat, moved that it be referred to a select committee, and the Speaker named Carpenter, Stuart, and Lincoln as the committee. Samuel Musick operated a ferry on Salt Creek, a Sangamon River tributary northeast of New Salem, and was ambitious to develop his business in pace with the county. The improvement was one every voter in north Sangamon County would favor, and Carpenter wanted some of the credit for himself. Saturday morning the committee reported an amendment, and the amended bill passed.

Immediately after passing Lincoln's bill the House enjoyed a respite from its routine of petitions for divorce, bills for the relief of citizens individually and collectively, petitions to Congress praying that money be appropriated to improve the state, measures declaring small creeks to be navigable streams, creating, discharging, and hearing reports of committees, laying bills on the table, and sitting as a committee of the whole House on important measures. The Senate joined them to elect a United States Senator. On a *viva voce* vote of 47 to 30, John McCracken Robinson, Democrat, was elected on December 20 to succeed himself. Lincoln joined the anti-Jacksonians in supporting Richard Montgomery Young, a milk-and-cider Jackson man.

On the third Monday morning of the session, three days before Christmas, the House felt twinges of conscience. Expecting to finish the session early in February, they had taken several afternoons off during the preceding week, and now voted overwhelmingly to begin work at 9 A.M. Having thus proved their industry, the House regularly adjourned for an hour at nine in the morning and began legislating at ten, until, a week later, they officially returned to the old hour.

Lincoln's bill of limitations on justices of the peace was rewritten in select committee and reported the day before Christmas. An amendment to the revised bill was proposed, whereupon another member moved that the whole matter be laid on the table until the fourth day of July, a waggish method of legislative slaughter. A lively debate sprang up between Lincoln and the amenders, who were mostly Whigs. The dispute ended when a Democrat, Stephen R. Rowan of Gallatin, moved commitment to still another special committee, which was done, Lincoln being named one of its three members. [27]

He voted against a Christmas holiday, lost, and spent the day talking politics. Early the next morning Lincoln learned the gratifying news that his toll bridge bill had been passed by the Senate. His other bill reappeared a day later, at the Saturday afternoon session. It had again been revised, and was referred to a fourth committee, this time "of the Whole House." The action of the committee of the whole on Monday afternoon was indecisive, and on motion of Stuart the bill was referred to still another special committee, of which Lincoln was not a member. Stuart, chairman of this committee, was so busy as member of other special committees and as chairman of the overworked standing committee on petitions, that Lincoln's bill did not reappear until nearly four weeks later, January 22, when it was reported with an amendment, then two days later passed, 39 to 7, and sent to the Senate. There, after all its vicissitudes in the House, it suffered indefinite postponement.

On Tuesday morning, January 6, after the House heard a long report from the committee on internal improvements, of which Dawson of Sangamon was chairman, Lincoln found and embraced an opportunity to address the House in that humorous style which was soon to bring him into prominence. Many days earlier the House had nominated one Samuel McHatton as surveyor of Schuyler County, and the Senate had appointed him. Now the House learned that no vacancy had existed. It was moved that the nomination "be vacated." This did not sound parliamentary. Lincoln stood up to discuss the question. The situation had its humorous aspect—two men legally chosen as simultaneous occupants of one position. The new surveyor, remarked Lincoln, could not legally oust the old one so long as the incumbent persisted in not dying. He therefore suggested that matters be let alone as they were, "so that if the old surveyor should hereafter conclude to die, there would be a new one ready without troubling the legislature." Stuart thought this approach unparliamentary also. He moved that the House rescind its nomination and ask the Senate to follow suit on the appointment. The matter was then laid on the table, an effective acceptance of Lincoln's proposal.[28]

This speech marks a turning point. For the previous five weeks the tall young man from New Salem had done little more than vote. He had been placed on three special committees. True, his two bills were doing well, but success with a brace of minor laws does not presage a brilliant political future. Any member could do as well. During the closing five weeks of the session, however, as though he had made an impression on the Speaker, Lincoln was named to serve on ten special committees, and was frequently recognized to make important motions. The prominence he tried unsuccessfully to gain as a parliamentary reformer could not be denied him as a wit. His personality had made him steadily more popular. As a story-teller he was already highly proficient, and his personal history, in a group containing many self-made men, established a rapport.[29] A lobbyist of the time who boarded at the same public house found him "raw-boned,

angular, features deeply furrowed, ungraceful, almost un-
couth; having little if any of that polish so important in society
life; and yet there was a magnetism and dash about the man
that made him a universal favorite. Underneath that rough
exterior—it was easy, too, to find out—dwelt a mind and a
heart of immense powers." [30]

Three days after Lincoln amused and led the House concerning the surveyor of Schuyler County, the lawmakers
considered President Jackson and the Bank of the United
States. It was their first extensive consideration of any political
issue of national importance since meeting. Party lines came
to the fore in a lengthy debate, and the president was upheld,
without the support of Stuart and Lincoln. The next afternoon,
January 10, Lincoln made in the House his first remarks on
an issue of national importance. He proposed a resolution
calling upon Illinois senators and representatives in Washington to exert themselves to obtain Congressional legislation
assigning to Illinois a portion (not less than twenty per cent)
of the money received from the sale of public lands in Illinois.
Another member thought this ought to be discussed by the
Committee of the Whole House, but Orlando Ficklin considered laying the resolution on the table a better disposition,
and the House agreed. This resolution, *per se*, was not important, for many successful resolutions called upon Congress,
vainly, for much greater favors. But Lincoln's public land
resolution does show that his outlook was widening, that his
recent votes on the issue of Jackson and the Bank had set him
to thinking seriously about larger affairs than toll bridges,
roads, and justices of the peace.

But local issues must be kept in mind too. Another election
would come in August, 1836, and Sangamon County constituents would be more concerned about legislative favors
than with Lincoln's public land views. Accordingly, on January 17 Lincoln presented "the petition of sundry citizens of
the counties of Sangamon, Morgan and Tazewell, praying the
organization of a new county out of said counties &c." He

moved that reading be dispensed with and reference made to the committee on petitions. This was done, and three weeks later the committee reported unfavorably and was sustained.[31] Before long the issue of county division was to be of prime importance to the New Salem area. But for this session the new member had done his duty.

The ambitious young solon was well launched politically. And by this time it was apparent that legislative service also offered pecuniary advantages. On December 19 he had collected a hundred dollars, with a larger sum due at the end of the session. Receiving a total of $258, of which $33 was travel allowance, Lincoln collected more than enough to pay off the loan which financed his first legislative appearance. The question of wages was raised in the House on January 21, when a member suggested that salaries of county officials be reduced. Lincoln and nearly all members voted to discuss it. A member proposed that the legislators cut their own pay, and the House quickly laid the matter on the table without a roll call.[32]

The salary issue, thanks to the speed with which it was dispatched, did not arouse public interest. Very few bills did as they went through the legislature. Illinois voters in general had one interest in legislative developments, and that was economy. Their philosophy of government was beautifully simple. The state must be governed upon minimum taxation, or new public officials would be chosen at the next election. Let the government authorize as many road and river improvements, canals, and railroads as they pleased, at somebody else's expense. Laws requiring increased taxation, however, would cause incumbents to fall like autumn leaves. In the sixteen years since 1818 Illinois politicians had learned this lesson well. During the 'twenties only a small part of the state revenue came from taxes on its own citizens,[33] a delightful custom voters wished to see made permanent. But the trend was against them, a harsh fact which made the voters even more watchful. Bills which created greatest public interest were those which spent, or threatened to spend, public funds. For Lincoln's first session these were the Illinois and Michigan Canal bill, the State Bank bill, and the measure creating five new circuit judgeships.[34] Neither canal nor bank bill actually appropriated money, and both, assisted by a swarm of lobbyists, passed by narrow margins. The circuit judge bill, while clearly costing money, passed easily, ample experience having shown that Supreme Court judges could no longer act efficiently as circuit judges. At least, the politicians could argue thus, while creating five new jobs.

A fourth measure, which aroused public interest on a smaller scale, dealt with funds for education. Given by the federal government public land and money to spend on schools, Illinois had not yet established a system of public education. Instead, the federal money had been "borrowed" and used for general state expenses. Friends of education banded together to end this game by forcing the legislature to spend education money for education. A lobby group calling itself the Illinois Institute of Education had been organized at Vandalia in 1833, and in November of 1834 succeeded in producing a series of county educational conventions. These groups chose delegates to a state convention which met in the capital on December 5. Sangamon County chose its six legislators and five other prominent citizens as delegates. The Vandalia convention produced a modest request that interest on the federal school money borrowed by the state be used for schools, but failed to stir up any great public interest. The lawmakers debated the issue for days. It was clear that free schools would mean taxes, and three education laws were passed which did no more than carry out the convention's request.[35]

At this period, with the fate of important measures like the canal and bank bills hanging in the balance, the capital's night life underwent a change. Comradely drinking and singing, parties, dances, theatricals gave way to business, and mild weather changed to bitter cold. Many a private decision was reached at tavern table and bar, but large questions were threshed out by candlelight in the House chamber as the lobby met each evening between dinner and bedtime. Representatives and senators met unhampered by official rules, to thresh things out with the aid of state officials, interested lobbyists, and small-fry politicians.

The session was drawing near its end. Bills were being passed in half dozen batches, and the House was speedily passing, or on rare occasions rejecting, bills received from the Senate, when on January 27 Lincoln gave notice of his intention to introduce "An act relative to a state road therein named." But Dawson of Sangamon, Democrat, again showed signs that the opposition feared Lincoln would become too popular at home. Dawson introduced the bill himself two days later. It became law, indicating that if Dawson had not intervened Lincoln could have converted two bills into law, out of three introduced. As chairman of the internal improvements committee, Dawson was the best man to expedite Lincoln's road bill, but Lincoln was not pleased. He retaliated with an encroachment of his own, staking out a credit claim on one of Dawson's bills, "An act to improve the navigation of the Sangamon river," by successfully moving, after the House passed the bill, that its title be changed to "An act to authorize a special election in Sangamon county." [36] Under Lincoln's title the bill became law.

On January 30 the question of reapportioning the state came up. The apportionment which gave Sangamon four representatives was only four years old, but the state was growing fast. A census was scheduled for 1835, which was bound to make reapportionment necessary unless the new figures were to be disregarded. A special committee had been studying the question of a special session for December. John T. Stuart reported a resolution asking that House and Senate "meet again at the Seat of Government on the first Monday of December, 1835." Webb of White County moved to lay the resolution on the table until July 4. Members from districts certain to lose strength enthusiastically supported the tabling motion, and the vote was 23 to 23. Having escaped the table, the resolution passed. Sangamon County would have increased representation under a reapportionment, and the Sangamon delegation voted in accordance with the county's interests.

The legislature was the great selector of public officials of Illinois. Voters were permitted to fill only four categories of state offices — governor, lieutenant governor, senators and representatives in the General Assembly. The last two did all the rest, from Supreme Court justices down through county surveyors. Elections had occurred at various times throughout the session, but a large number of selections not yet made were cleaned up at a joint session Tuesday afternoon, February 10. During the last week of the session attendance was often low, but for the elections nearly all members appeared. By an overwhelming majority, including Lincoln, Jesse Burgess Thomas, former United States Senator, was elected attorney general to replace Ninian W. Edwards, resigned. Five state's attorneys were selected for five judicial districts, among them S. A. Douglass (Lincoln voting against) and O. B. Ficklin (Lincoln voting for). A crowd of members, including Lincoln, walked out while the warden of the penitentiary was being chosen. Three judges of probate were elected by ballot as still fewer remained. Elective functions completed, the Senate filed upstairs, and the session was nearly over.

When the House doorkeeper blew out the candles on Friday night, February 13, the General Assembly having adjourned *sine die*, the Honorable Abraham Lincoln had performed about every function a House member could, in the ordinary run of legislating, except serving as chairman of an important committee, presiding over the Committee of the Whole House, and acting on a Senate-House conference committee. Not until the last day but one did he call for the Yeas and Nays. He did so twice on February 12. It is true but misleading to generalize that Lincoln usually voted with Stuart. A breakdown of their votes on measures, when both were present,

shows that Stuart and Lincoln voted together a hundred and
one times, and Lincoln voted against his mentor twenty-six
times. Frequently Stuart would be absent, working in committee, when roll was called. On the few occasions when
Lincoln was absent, Stuart was on the floor. On no roll call
were both absent, indicating that they worked as a team.
When public officials were elected by calling the roll of the
House, Lincoln differed with Stuart only once.

Since Stuart, Whig floor leader, had Congressional ambitions which he hoped would ere long remove him from
Vandalia, the co-operation of the two Whigs in answering roll
call hints that Stuart was grooming the lanky young man to
succeed him as Whig leader in the House. Of significance also
is the recently discovered fact that a few bills not Lincoln's
were written in his hand, and introduced by others.[37] Probably
this custom began because his handwriting was exceptionally
legible. His proficiency in penmanship, not his knowledge,
was being used. But the habit was valuable, for it made
Lincoln a more useful member, imparted skills and established
contacts which could easily grow into authorship of legislative
bills on a wide scale.

A further interesting aspect of Lincoln's first session was
perhaps the inception of his habit of writing anonymous letters
to the press. As a Whig officeholder he was naturally well
known to Simeon Francis, editor of the Springfield Whig
paper, the *Sangamo Journal*. In this paper appeared reports
from Vandalia which might have been written by Lincoln.
On December 13 the *Journal* printed a short letter from
Vandalia under the caption "From Our Correspondent." [38]
The report was a brief summary of the important measures
before the legislature, in a style resembling Lincoln's. Men-
tioning five bills, "Our Correspondent" was not sure about
the prospects of three, but thought the other two would fail,
a prediction in which he was mistaken. Two more letters
appeared in the *Journal* before adjournment.[39] The third
letter merely reported progress, but the second was a heavily

humorous account of House Democrats arguing among themselves over resolutions approving Jackson's bank policy. While Democrats squabbled, wrote "Our Correspondent," Aristocrats were silent. "They held in, knowing that a word from an Aristocrat could effect nothing except probably, to unite the Democrats. . . . The thing was funny, and we Aristocrats enjoyed it 'hugely,' as Tristram Shandy says."

Vandalia merchants watched with sorrow the rapid exodus of the capital's transient population, and the doldrums speedily set in. Governor Duncan went off to more comfortable quarters at his home in Jacksonville. Lincoln, with more than a hundred dollars in his pocket, boarded the first stage to Springfield alongside Stuart, Carpenter, and Dawson. Descending at New Salem at the end of a cold ride in twenty-below-zero weather, the tall young legislator triumphantly shook hands, renewed acquaintances, and told stories of the mysteries of government. With a successful season of public service to his credit, he cut a larger figure than he did a year earlier. Postal and surveying activities were resumed, but with a difference. Lincoln had found his profession. Previous contacts with the practice of law had been tentative and timorous; he doubted his ability to become a lawyer. After making laws for two and a half months, and intimately associating with the state's leading lawyers, the calling no longer seemed unattainable and he began to study seriously. Stuart, his political mentor, encouraged him to study law and became his legal mentor as well. From Stuart, Lincoln, as he recalled later in writing an autobiography, borrowed law books and "went at it in good earnest. He studied with nobody. He still mixed in the surveying to pay board and clothing bills. When the Legislature met, the law books were dropped, but were taken up again at the end of the session." [40]

Politics again came to the fore in the late autumn. On November 10, Lincoln wrote a letter to Governor Duncan recommending appointment of Levi Davis of Vandalia as auditor, and Davis was installed when the legislators drifted into Vandalia for the special session arranged the preceding January. They approached through heavy snow, and found the capital lovely under a thick blanket of white. The cluster of log cabins with smoking chimneys presented a picture suitable for modern Christmas cards. The square, however, had been too much traveled to be anything but a mass of churned gray. And the honorable members, once inside the state house, regretted that last winter's mildness had not returned. The building was more dilapidated than ever. Cracks ran down the walls. The north wall bulged out several inches and the west wall had sunk an inch or two. Piles of sifted snow adorned the Senate floor, new in 1834, but now sunk half a foot at the center.[41]

Fewer lobbyists, office-seekers, and social visitors appeared for the short special session, an absence more than compensated for by a swarm of Democratic politicians. Little Stephen A. Douglass, now a state's attorney, had begun the process of convincing Illinois Democrats that organization would reduce internal strife and produce more Whig defeats. The first state political convention in Illinois history began in the House chamber on opening day, after the legislature had hastily organized and adjourned.

Vice-President Martin Van Buren had been nominated Democratic presidential candidate at Baltimore in May, and the Douglass objective was to obtain endorsement of "Little Matty," select a pledged electoral ticket, produce a seductive address to the people, and force into line the milk-and-cider Jackson men. Whig strategy against Van Buren called for support of whichever of three candidates, Daniel Webster, William Henry Harrison, or Hugh Lawson White, was strongest in each state. In Illinois it was White of Tennessee. The anonymous Vandalia correspondent of the *Sangamo Journal* was inspired to write a small volume reporting and reproving the opposition convention. Democratic "dictation" and the squirming of anti-convention Democrats so inspired the reporter that he wrote more than the *Journal* could print on schedule. Long letters on the subject appeared in February, 1836, after the legislature had adjourned.[42]

On December 12, 1835, "Our Correspondent" pictured a crowd of Democrats in town. "There are no White men here from a distance without business," he wrote, "while the hotels are lined with ruffle-shirted Vannies. There is no one here whose sole business it is to puff Judge White; consequently I seldom hear his name except when I go among the people, where (God be praised!) I hear nothing else." He wrote gaily of Democratic arguments over a convention president, and waggishly depicted, as a sample of "British aggression," the activity of Ebenezer Peck, "late of Canada, now of Chicago," who insisted on the virtues of organization.[43]

On the second day, December 8, Governor Duncan's message was read to the assembled House. It was brief, and called for a brief session. In addition to reapportionment, he directed attention to defects in the Illinois and Michigan Canal and State Bank acts, both passed in 1835. Modern legislatures, meeting in special session, act only on those matters for which the governor calls them together; but members of the Ninth General Assembly, with a lively sense of the approaching campaign of 1836, speedily began acting on every subject which came to mind. The special session was distinguishable from regular sessions only by its comparative brevity. In addition to the three bills asked by the executive, House and Senate each added more than a hundred of their own. From the number of corporations authorized it would seem that a large portion of the state's inhabitants were interested in a new railroad company, canal company, or insurance company.

John T. Stuart, his ambitions now fixed on a seat in Congress, played a less active part than usual, while the voice of Abraham Lincoln was heard as frequently as it had been during the last half of the regular session. Though he introduced only one bill of his own, an act regarding insolvent debtors (which passed the House but stuck in the Senate), he reported two Sangamon County road bills at the behest of petitioners,

Joseph Duncan

and as chairman of a special committee shepherded through the House a bill incorporating the Beardstown and Sangamon Canal Company. Lincoln served on five special committees, and was chairman of three. His popularity with the Speaker, James Semple, held until mid-session, when a United States Senator was elected *vice* the late Elias Kent Kane. News of Kane's death, wrote the capital correspondent of the *Sangamo Journal*, threw Vandalia into a state of "continual commotion." Nine candidates offered themselves at once. But "he whose prospects seem brightest in one hour, is off the track by the next." Semple was the leading candidate for eight ballots, but lost on the twelfth to W. L. D. Ewing. Lincoln did not once vote for Semple; instead he helped elect Ewing, and was not popular with the Speaker during the closing three weeks of the session. Writing a fascinating report of the election to the Springfield editor, "Our Correspondent" pictured Semple's defeat as a blow to convention Democrats. "Our friends," he concluded, "have had but two shots at that convention — but each of those has brought a pigeon. These two, mind ye, are the large fowls: they'll kill them off faster when once they get among the little ones." [44]

As a parliamentary tactician Lincoln kept a close eye on the interests of Sangamon County, outshining Stuart in that respect. When a Senate bill reached the House, for example, requiring the county to bridge the Sangamon River, Lincoln successfully moved an amendment providing a second bridge near New Salem. But the Senate refused to accept the amendment. Faced with the responsibility of killing the bridge, Lincoln astutely engineered removal of his amendment, and the bill became law.[45]

On the important reapportionment measure Lincoln's course was somewhat puzzling. He offered an apportionment figure which would add only twelve new members, while Sangamon County stood to gain heavily under a larger increase. Probably, knowing that a large membership was certain, he wished to stake out an economy claim which would be useful on the hustings the following summer. The new apportionment law provided a House of ninety-one members and gave Sangamon seven representatives instead of four. Lincoln's seat was thus made doubly secure.

Important also was the fact that he collected $162 for his second session labors, and materially advanced his political education and prospects. The Democratic state convention had completed its labors the evening of the second day, but its influence lingered. As soon as possible a House Whig introduced a resolution denouncing the convention system as "anti-republican." A Democrat moved to lay it on the table "until the 4th day of July next." Lincoln and the resolution's author called for the Yeas and Nays, and on the table it went, 33 to 19. In the Senate, where Whigs and Democrats were more evenly matched, the Whigs jammed through, 13 to 12, a resolution nominating White for president, by the clever expedient of labeling White a better Democrat than Van Buren, winning the support of five milk-and-cider senators who abhorred the convention system. Democrats raged at this successful maneuver. Late in the session the House Democrats exploded a long resolution branding White an associate of nullifiers and traitors, denouncing the opposition's assumption of "the ancient and honorable name of *Whig*," and declaring "the most perfect confidence" in Van Buren. Whigs fought back with every possible parliamentary device, seeking to prevent a vote. Dawson of Sangamon, backsliding into the Whig camp, Stuart, and Lincoln figured prominently in the persistent delaying action. But in vain; the anti-White resolutions passed, 30 to 20.[46]

Two weeks later, January 18, 1836, the special session ended, and lawmakers journeyed home in weather mild as spring. The Springfield stage carried an unhappy man. William Carpenter, Democrat, was disgusted at the apostasy of Dawson, chairman of the important internal improvements committee. Stuart and Lincoln were delighted at Dawson's switch. During the session all three had supported the popular new movement to make Illinois great and wealthy through large-scale internal improvements. "Our Correspondent's" letters to the editor dealt in detail with dastardly Democratic efforts to thwart the will of the people as the new canal bill wended its tortuous way through House and Senate. The legislature had just authorized seventeen new railroads, all to be privately financed—perfectly safe legislation. Perhaps the next Sangamon County delegation, nine strong, might be able to use the internal improvements issue to carry out a grandiose scheme for Sangamon.

PART THREE
THE LONG NINE

THE LONG NINE

SHORTLY after Lincoln returned to New Salem as an experienced legislator to greet his constituents, the *Illinois Advocate* in Vandalia proudly announced on February 3 the end of its journalistic monopoly. Soon, said the *Advocate*, there would be two additional papers for the campaign of 1836, a Whig sheet, and the *Illinois State Register and Vandalia Republican* for Van Buren. The Democratic *Register* appeared on February 12, hailed by the *Advocate* as an "able assistant" in the fight to elect Jackson's chosen political heir. But by the end of March, John York Sawyer, public printer and editor of the *Advocate*, was dead of pneumonia, and his paper was swallowed by the *Register*, William Walters, editor and proprietor.[1] The Whig paper, dubbed *Free Press* and edited by an unsuccessful legislative aspirant named William Hodge, appeared in May, and fought through the campaign before changing its name to *Free Press and Illinois Whig*.

The presidential campaign, vigorously begun in Illinois by the cross fire between House and Senate over Van Buren and White, and by editorial give-and-take in the partisan press, waxed warmer throughout spring, summer, and autumn. Lincoln followed the Whig line as a confirmed White man. With his Whig colleagues, the young legislator campaigned so effectively that Van Buren lost Sangamon County by a heavy vote. But more important to the local Whigs than the presidential canvass was the legislative race. The two did not conflict, for the legislative election came August 1, the presidential election November 7. And a good showing for White in November was sought to enhance the prestige of the Sangamon Whigs.

Abraham Lincoln, politically confident, enlarged his nonpolitical activities. Again a working surveyor, in February he laid out the town of Petersburg, hard by New Salem; surveyed another town, Huron, in March, and a third, Albany, in June. New Salem residents moved steadily into the new village of Petersburg, and soon the New Salem post office was closed. In March Lincoln was certified in court as a person of good character, a preliminary to admission to the practice of law; and he made a few cautious investments in land.[2]

It was in March, also, that Lincoln announced his candidacy for re-election to the legislature, and in June wrote his campaign platform for publication in the *Sangamo Journal*. William Carpenter became postmaster of Springfield and did not run again, nor did Stuart, a candidate for Congress. Dawson, now openly a Whig, did enter the race. Thus, with seven seats to be filled, only two candidates sought re-election. Candidates appeared in such numbers that voters called for guidance, asking the aspirants to "show their hands." "Agreed," wrote Lincoln in a New Salem cabin. "Here's mine."

Nothing was easier for him than writing letters to the press. He favored universal adult suffrage, internal improvements paid for "by distributing the proceeds of the sales of the public lands," and Hugh L. White for president. As representative, he would carry out the will of Sangamon County. In matters on which the wishes of his constituents could not be known, he would do what his own judgment taught him would "best advance their interests." Of more than a dozen announced candidates, only five wrote their principles, and Lincoln's letter was by far the ablest and most succinct.[3] Other candidates included William F. Elkin, former representative and unsuccessful senatorial aspirant; Ninian W. Edwards, recently attorney general of Illinois, resigned; Andrew McCormick, who finished sixth in 1834; Richard Quinton, Democrat, nosed out by Stuart in that year; John Calhoun, Democrat, former county surveyor and employer of Lincoln; and a host of newcomers.

Canards began to fly in June, and the whole of July was spent on the hustings. Serious candidates of both parties (not including casuals like the individual known only as Yancy, who polled twelve votes on election day), arranged through the Springfield papers a series of political meetings which enabled every candidate to be heard in all sections of the county. The politicians traveled on horseback from one grove or town to the next, and each made a speech. "Mr. Lincoln," wrote one of his colleagues, "took a leading part . . . , manifesting skill and tact in offensive and defensive debates, presenting his arguments with great force and ability, and boldly attacking the . . . positions taken by opposing candidates." [4]

The Whigs were greatly assisted by an extensive revolt among milk-and-cider Democrats, who, disgusted with Van Buren as Jackson's heir, had begun kicking over the traces early in 1835. The canvass began at Springfield, then the caravan rode west, north, east, south, west, ending at Springfield on July 30. A measure much discussed was the unpopular, "undemocratic" "Little Bull" law, passed at the last session. But Lincoln was safe; he had voted against it. On election day he ran highest among the seventeen who received votes, and the entire Whig slate won. A Whig was elected senator; and since the holdover senator, Archer Gray Herndon, was also a Whig, Sangamon County had a representation of nine Whigs in Senate and House, a group large enough to accomplish things if united and directed toward a common goal. Before the party of nine reached Vandalia in December, steps were taken to provide a common objective.

Meanwhile Lincoln was licensed to practice law in Illinois, and had tried and lost his first case in Springfield before the Sangamon County Circuit Court.

Vandalia, by law capital of Illinois until 1840, lay far to the north of Kaskaskia; but it was still in the southern part of the state. Population trends of the early 'thirties clearly indicated that central and northern Illinois were destined to be the populous areas, and agitation for a northerly movement of the capital was inevitable. The legislature in 1833, seeing an opportunity to placate public opinion at no cost and at the same time strike a blow at the expanding north, provided for a vote on capital relocation at the next general election, August, 1834.

When this measure became law Springfield advanced its claim, declaring that no other town could rival the central location of the seat of Sangamon County. Sangamon promoters prepared for the election by arranging a convention of northern counties which met at Rushville, northwest of Beardstown, near but not in Sangamon, in April, 1834. Twelve counties sent delegates, who resolved that citizens should vote for Springfield. Efforts to displace Springfield with Alton, Peoria, and "Geographical Centre" were defeated, and a long "Address to the People" recited the reasons for moving the capital from Vandalia to Springfield. The act providing for the election, alleged the address, was unfairly drawn. Northern voters could choose one of four sites, while southerners had but two choices. This effort to "divide and conquer" could be beaten only by united northern support of Springfield. A long *Sangamo Journal* editorial of two months later detailed Springfield's qualifications, and pointed out why Alton and Peoria did not merit a second thought.[5]

Letters to the editor in numerous newspapers kept the subject warm. Springfield's champions directed their strongest blows at Alton, the Mississippi River town which thought itself destined to challenge St. Louis as a metropolis. But on election day Springfield ran third, narrowly nosed out by Vandalia and Alton. Only these three received sustained support, and Springfield complained that if all counties had voted, and northern votes had not been diverted by the skulduggery of placing Peoria, Jacksonville, and Geographical Centre on the list, Springfield would have received twice the total given to Alton.[6] Nothing could be done about relocation during Lincoln's first two sessions. The south was still too strong. Action must await reapportionment, after which northern counties like Cook would have more than one-sixth of a representative — in 1836 Cook County elected three men to the House.

A fortnight before the Sangamon delegation left for the seat of government, a public meeting on the subject of internal improvements was held in Springfield. Grandiose hopes of navigability of the Sangamon River having run aground in 1832, the county required a railroad to get its agricultural surplus to market. Efforts of 1835 to build a road by means of private capital came to nothing, and the county, perforce, placed its hopes on a railroad financed by the state treasury. The public meeting on internal improvements therefore evoked enthusiastic support. The *Sangamo Journal* admonished on the day of the Springfield meeting:

> It is now time TO ACT. The present we consider the proper moment to invite the attention of our fellow citizens in other Counties to the proposed Internal Improvements Convention [planned to assemble in Vandalia early in December]. It is now, we believe, . . . a certainty, that the Convention will be held. It is not a party measure, and all our citizens can cordially unite in one vigorous effort to secure the adoption of a system of Internal Improvements for this State, which is so much needed, so much desired, and so absolutely necessary to its prosperity.[7]

The meeting resolved that Illinois required and demanded broad internal improvements, to be financed by borrowed money, not by taxation; adopted a seven-point program to be submitted to the Vandalia convention; and appointed sixteen delegates. No representative or senator was named a delegate; the slate was bipartisan, including John T. Stuart and Colonel Thomas Mather, Whigs; George Forquer, John Calhoun, and Robert Allen, Democrats. Nothing was said at the meeting about capital relocation. The absence of the county's lawmakers from the delegate list was strange. A week later a *Journal* editorial on the approaching legislative session spoke of the internal improvement need, of judicial reform, of a United States Senator to be elected, of better road laws, but ignored capital relocation.[8] Sangamon County viewed internal improvements as something to be sought for the sake of transportation and economic advance, and secretly, as a bargaining instrument which might make Springfield the permanent capital of Illinois.

Abraham Lincoln, addressing his Springfield constituents as he opened his campaign for re-election, pointed to the last legislature as the one which pulled the state out of debt. The claim was well-founded. Legislative parsimony, coupled with that national prosperity which enabled the Jackson administration to pay off all the national debt and pile up a surplus, had produced, "for once," a treasury surplus in Vandalia. And Illinois expected nearly a million dollars from Washington when the federal government "distributed" or "deposited" the national surplus.[9]

Vandalia, like state and nation, was booming. Land speculation was so popular that any traveler from out of the state was automatically taken for a land agent and approached as such. One literary sojourner who passed through Vandalia in the summer of 1836 found the capital disappointing and unprepossessing:

> Its site is an elevated, undulating tract upon the west bank of the Kaskaskia, and was once heavily timbered, as are now its suburbs. The streets are of liberal breadth —. . . enclosing an elevated public square nearly in the centre of the village, which a little expenditure of time and money might render a delightful promenade. The public edifices are very inconsiderable, consisting of an ordinary structure of brick for legislative purposes; a similar building originally erected as a banking establishment, but now occupied by the offices of the state authorities; a Presbyterian Church, with cupola and bell, besides a number of lesser buildings for purposes of worship and education. A handsome structure of stone for a bank is, however, in progress, which, when completed, with other public buildings in contemplation, will add much to the aspect of the place. Here also is a land-office for the district, and the Cumberland Road is permanently located and partially constructed to the place. . . . We are told that the first legislators who assembled in session at this place sought their way through the neighbouring prairies as the mariner steers over the trackless ocean, by his knowledge of the cardinal points. Judges and lawyers came pouring in from opposite

directions, as wandering tribes assemble to council; and many were the tales of adventure and mishap related at their meeting.[10]

This traveler, despite his unflattering description of the village of 1836, saw Vandalia as a future metropolis with an imposing record of progress already to its credit. Commercial establishments, sharing the general optimism, were more numerous than ever. Charles Prentice, merchant, sold out at a profit early in 1836, opened a new store in April ("Dry Goods, Hard Ware, Queensware, Groceries, Cutlery, Glassware, tinware, etc. . . . , will be sold uncommonly low for cash, or in exchange for Wheat, live hogs, pork, bacon, butter, Beeswax, tallow, beefhides, deer skins, furs, etc."), moved into enlarged quarters in December, and ran an advertisement more than a column long. The number of physicians had doubled, and skilled laborers were in demand. A summer advertisement ran:

> The undersigned having contracted to erect several large buildings in the town of Vandalia, will give immediate employment to any number of carpenters and bricklayers that will remove to this place without delay. Two dollars per day will be given for first rate hands and ready pay in all cases. Apply immediately to A. & H. Lee, T. B. Hickman, J. Taylor & Co., D. B. Waterman & Co.[11]

True, improvements were wanted almost anywhere one looked. The road across the Kaskaskia had been nearly impassable in August. Bridge repairs, paid for by private subscription and the town trustees, were under way. A writer who signed himself "Vandalia" complained in September of the "infamous Stage carriages . . . tolerated on all lines" running to the capital. The Democratic newspaper ran out of paper in November, giving the Whigs a temporary monopoly.[12] Any one who doubted, however, that needed improvements were being carried forward had but to look at the public square, where a new capitol was rising.

The second state house, ruinous when the legislature adjourned in January, threatened to fall down in June. The west wall had sunk four inches, and the north wall bulged out almost a foot. The floor of the Senate chamber, nine inches down at the center, somewhat resembled a modern indoor running track. A Methodist congregation accustomed to meet in the state house refused to return. The old bank building, which housed state offices, was almost as bad. A crisis in public buildings was at hand. Governor Duncan hoped, as late as August, that the capitol could be repaired. But Secretary of State Field, Auditor Davis, and Treasurer Dement, assured by mechanics that repairs were impossible, convinced him that a new state house was necessary. The legislature had authorized no such building, but neither had they in 1824 when the now decrepit second state house was put up to replace the burned wooden capitol.[13]

Vandalia citizens, intent on retaining the seat of government, with Alexander P. Field, Levi Davis, and James T. B. Stapp, former auditor, at the head of the movement, pledged $500 by individual subscriptions and induced Governor Duncan to assign $5,000 from the state contingent fund to get the work started. The two decrepit old buildings were torn down and salvaged materials were used in the new building or sold. Excavation began in the center of the public square, and a stone foundation was laid in late August.[14] A local joiner, John Taylor, assisted by William Hodge, editor of the Whig paper, hastily drew plans for a plain two-story brick building deemed large enough to house the legislature and most state officials for decades to come. The whole project, as in 1824, was based on faith that the state would pay for the completed capitol.

Throughout autumn the public square was thronged with workers cleaning brick from the old buildings, hauling new brick from a local kiln, shoveling sand dug from the river, toiling day and night in fair weather and foul. Wagons from St. Louis hauled timbers, planks, flooring, glass, putty, hardware to be unloaded and installed.[15] By late November, when legislators began arriving by stage and registering at Robert

Blackwell's New White House, Abner Flack's Vandalia Hotel (formerly Charter's Tavern), or the "New Hotel" at the Sign of the Green Tree, the dignitaries peered with interest at the littered lot on the west side of the square where the old state house stood, and at the new capitol in the center, surrounded by apparatus of construction. Vandalia could congratulate itself that the building was erected by December 5, the opening date of the Tenth General Assembly, though much remained to be done within. Surely such industry would not be spurned, and such energy ignored, by moving the seat of government.

Innkeepers of Vandalia had no cause for complaint in December, unless it was to regret that their establishments were not more commodious. Prices were up and customers numerous. An enlarged legislature was assembling for a session destined to be the longest yet held. Great measures would be before it, augmenting the crowd of lobbyists and hangers-on. So numerous were these that the social season began badly; few wives could find accommodations. Only three or four appeared during the whole month, and they became "heartily sick of the place." [16] Workmen would be needed all winter at the state house to finish the interior. The state internal improvements convention brought a swarm of interested parties, many of whom would remain until the last word had been said on the subject in House, Senate, and Council of Revision. Government itself was a source of custom. Officials deprived of office space by the building program could not move into the new capitol, for the builders had concentrated on the second floor in order to finish in time for the legislative session, and had left the first floor interior to be completed while debate resounded upstairs.

Joseph Duncan was back from his Jacksonville home, angrier than ever at the public acts of his former friend Jackson, and prepared to say so officially. Looking over the roster of the legislature, the governor found that the House contained a heavy majority of new faces — 66 novice legislators — the re-

sult of reapportionment and popular detestation of the Little
Bull law. Only sixteen veterans of the 1834 and '35 sessions returned, while nine who had been members in 1832 or earlier
were back. In the Senate, to which twenty-eight had been
elected in 1836, there were twelve new faces, five re-elected
senators, and eleven new senators who had advanced from the
House.

The arrival of so many new men made the lines of party
alignment even more confused than usual. How would these
novices vote? No one could be sure until the situation developed, but Duncan could expect trouble, for Jackson's party
had just won a presidential election, and floaters would gravi-
tate in that direction. As legislation began, the House was
discovered to contain 36 Democrats, 8 questionable Democrats, 19 Whigs, 4 questionable Whigs, and 24 members who
might go either way. These last held the balance of power, and
only four of them tended to vote Whig regularly. The Senate
contained a nominal Democratic majority, but many who
called themselves Democrats were old Jackson men in revolt
against the new-fangled Douglass-convention, party-line
system, and voted with the Whigs so often that the minority
party controlled the Senate.[17]

No less difficult than the task of distinguishing Whig from
Democrat was that of picking out, among the stream of men
who walked carefully through the debris of construction and
entered the new capitol, the men of ability and promise from
those who would never again hold a post of public trust. There
were plenty of both varieties in Vandalia as December arrived. No Illinois legislature before or since contained so many
men of future distinction.[18] Most of these were in the House.

Little Stephen Douglass, now twenty-three, stood at the
head of Morgan County's six-man delegation, all Democrats
but one. A first-termer, he was already a leader, prepared to
play a major rôle in the session.

The lone Whig of the Morgan six was handsome, belligerent
John J. Hardin, twenty-six, aristocratic Kentuckian, educated

lawyer, former prosecuting attorney, and an opponent of headlong internal improvements. Hardin had the ability and convictions of the successful politician, but lacked the wiles. A ready orator, he habitually spent the first fifteen minutes of a speech in a combination stammer and stumble, but plowed ahead regardless, and settled down to rugged eloquence.

James Shields

Another youngster was Augustus Chaplin French, Democrat, New Hampshire native, lawyer of moderate abilities and no polish, without capacities for leadership, inveterate teller of Munchausen-like stories, who was to astonish his colleagues by being elected, in 1846, the first Yankee governor of Illinois, and to surprise them again by becoming the first Illinois governor to win re-election.

James Shields, twenty-six, Democrat, born in Ireland, Kas-

kaskia lawyer, possessed more than his share of the pugnacity
native to the "auld sod." A student of languages as well as of
law, he was also a professional soldier who spared no pains to
look the part. Handsome, erect, black-mustached, Shields
had been seriously wounded in the Florida campaigns, was
popular and extremely combative. He was later to come close
to crossing swords, literally, with Abraham Lincoln, and still
later to set an American record by being elected United States
Senator from three states, Illinois, Minnesota, and Missouri.

A fifth newcomer was Usher Ferguson Linder of Coles
County, of Whiggish persuasion, Kentuckian, lawyer, who had
been in Illinois one year. Tall and gangling, dandified in
dress, fond of the bottle, a witty and powerful speaker, Linder
rapidly acquired influence and was elected attorney general at
mid-session. His touchstone of conduct was to deliver a speech
at every opportunity. In old age Linder was to write his
reminiscences of his political colleagues, describing nearly all
as paragons of oratory, while secretly believing that he could
beat the lot.

Linder was not a Lincoln man. Nor was John Alexander
McClernand of Shawneetown, twenty-four, lawyer, first-
termer, Black Hawk War veteran, future Congressman and
general, whose eloquence quickly brought him influence. A
third vigorous opponent of Lincoln's program was little John
Dement of Vandalia, recently treasurer, who entered the
House to protect Vandalia's future.

Steadfastly on Lincoln's side was John Hogan, thirty-one,
first-termer, native of County Cork, former itinerant Methodist
preacher and cobbler, turned Belleville merchant. Short, red-
faced, garrulous, companionable, his loud voice was often
heard hymning the glories of internal improvements.

Edwin B. Webb of White County, thirty-four, lawyer,
second-termer, was a Virginia gentleman and warm friend of
Captain Lincoln. Called "Bat" because of his small figure,
elegant garb and manners, Webb worked for caution and
sanity in internal improvements.[19]

Lincoln's really important support came from the Sangamon delegation of nine Whigs, seven in the House, two in the Senate. Dubbed "the Long Nine" on arrival in Vandalia, they attracted attention as the largest delegation, the most united, and the tallest. Some of the Long Nine were men of average height, while two, Lincoln and Andrew McCormick, were giants. The total height of the Sangamon nine was exactly fifty-four feet. The Long Nine stood out in political experience and ability as they did in altitude. Lincoln, their leader, was with one exception the youngest. He had stepped into the shoes of John T. Stuart and had not yet proved his capacity for political management. Among his Sangamon colleagues in the House were two men of greater experience, John Dawson and Dan Stone.

Dawson, forty-five, Virginian, veteran of the War of 1812, in which he was wounded, captured by Indians, and held prisoner in Canada until ransomed by friends, had come to Sangamon County in 1827, staked out a farm, begotten ten children, served as captain in the Black Hawk War, and been elected to the legislature in 1830 and 1834.

Dan Stone, thirty-six, Vermonter, had acquired a college education and come west to Cincinnati, where he practiced law, was a member of the city council, and served in the Ohio legislature. He arrived in Springfield in 1833, and quickly established himself as a man of parts. Stone was an enthusiastic tree fancier, debater, and opponent of slavery.

William F. Elkin, oldest of the Long Nine, was forty-five and the father of fifteen children. Kentucky-born, he reached the Sangamon region in 1825 after stops in Ohio and Indiana, established a farm, and was elected to the legislature in 1828.

Youngest of the Long Nine — younger than Lincoln by two months — was Ninian W. Edwards. Vain and reserved, Edwards was not popular in the legislature, and hence did not acquire influence consistent with his merits. "Constitutionally an aristocrat," wrote a colleague of Edwards, "he hated democracy . . . as the devil is said to hate holy water." [20]

Robert L. Wilson, thirty-one, Pennsylvanian, was a self-made lawyer who reached Sangamon County by way of Ohio and Kentucky in 1833, and practiced law in the village of Athens, ten miles north of Springfield. The 1836 campaign was Wilson's first political venture.

Only slightly more experienced was Andrew McCormick of Springfield, thirty-five, stonecutter, a man almost as tall as Lincoln and weighing nearly three hundred pounds. A native of Tennessee, McCormick was forced when only fourteen to become head of a family of nine. These dependents he supported successfully, brought them to Sangamon County in 1829, then went adventuring in the Galena lead region, fought in the Indian wars, came to Springfield in 1833, married, and begat the first of ten children. A candidate for the legislature in 1834, McCormick had finished in sixth place; in 1836 he was seventh, but was elected.

The Long Nine had two men in the Senate, Job Fletcher and Archer G. Herndon. Fletcher, forty-three, Virginian, War of 1812 veteran, farmer, father of seven, was among the earliest to plant in the rich Sangamon soil, arriving in 1819. Besides farming, Fletcher taught school and served as the county's first justice of the peace. He had served one term (1826–28) in the House, one session in the Senate (1835–36), and had been defeated in three campaigns (1822, 1828, 1830).

Archer G. Herndon, forty-one, Virginian, Springfield tavernkeeper, had reached Sangamon County in 1821, almost as early as Fletcher. His eldest son, William Henry Herndon, was nearly eighteen, and ready to enter Illinois College at Jacksonville. Strongly pro-slavery, Archer Herndon's political allegiance was a mystery to friend and foe. He was Whig or Democrat at will, but mostly Democrat. At the moment he was acting with the Whigs. Herndon's Senate seat marked his first success in politics; in 1830 and 1832 he had been defeated.[21]

Besides Herndon and Fletcher, and holdover senators like Cyrus Edwards, the Senate contained only two notables.

Orville Hickman Browning of Quincy, new member and staunch friend of Lincoln, was starting his long public career. Robert K. McLaughlin, one of the founders of Vandalia, former treasurer and member of both houses, was back in the Senate to assist John Dement in the fight against the capital removers.

Important men were seen and heard also among the crowd of lobbyists. Gurdon Saltonstall Hubbard, New Englander, former representative from Danville, now of Chicago, Indian trader and pioneer, master of Indian lore, Black Hawk War veteran, was in the capital "with some axes to grind." As a commissioner of the proposed Illinois and Michigan Canal, appointed by Governor Duncan in 1835, Hubbard's interest was obvious; he hoped, however, to persuade the legislature to forget the canal and build a railroad. During the session he entertained the lawmakers by performing an authentic Winnebago Indian war dance in costume.

John T. Stuart, internal improvements convention delegate, defeated for Congress in 1836, was present to aid the Long Nine in their ambitious projects and to enhance his Congressional prospects for 1838. "Cheerful, social and good-humored," Stuart was popular and very influential. Sometimes he was referred to as the handsomest man in the state, sometimes dubbed "Jerry Sly" because of his "great powers of sly management and intrigue."

Also a prominent supporter of the Sangamon County delegation was Archibald Williams of Quincy, former senator and in 1836 a candidate for the United States Senate. Tall, angular, awkward, he was considered the homeliest man in the state. A Kentuckian, self-made lawyer, clear thinker, he was politically a backsliding Democrat, and associated himself during the session with Lincoln. As a former senator, Williams had access to both houses, and spent so much time conferring with Lincoln in the House that some historians have taken him for a member. Visitors, seeing Williams and Lincoln near Lincoln's seat in a rear corner (from which the Sangamon leader could watch the House carefully and get out quickly to mend a fence), heads together in earnest conversation, were moved to inquire, "Who in hell are those two ugly men?" [22]

Looking over the new state house before the convening of the Tenth General Assembly, the honorable members from Sangamon were gratified, and Vandalia partisans were shocked, to find the unfinished building too small for the expanded membership. The ambitious builders, never having dealt with a House of ninety-one, had not made the chamber large enough for 1836; much less would it do for 1856. Therefore the new building did not constitute a strong argument for keeping the government in Vandalia. Dodging workmen, Lincoln and Stuart examined the second floor. The House chamber occupied the west end, the Senate chamber the east, and between the two, at the end of a central hall, was a room for committees and clerks. Both chambers had a spectators' gallery built as a balcony at the rear, reached by an ascending staircase. Desks, tables, chairs, and sandbox spittoons were old friends. They had been moved from the old capitol, while chairs and a few tables had been bought from local merchants and crowded in for the twenty-six additional representatives.

Monday morning, December 5, the legislature began work, but under difficulties. "The plastering . . . is not yet dry," said a local paper, and the legislative chambers were "consequently most uncomfortable, if not unsafe, tenements." [23] Dawson called the House to order, temporary officers were chosen, and adjournment quickly agreed upon. In the afternoon a Speaker was elected. The candidates were the veteran James Semple, John Dement, favorite of Vandalia's partisans, and Newton Cloud, the Morgan County preacher. Putting up no candidate of their own, the Whigs supported Cloud, who failed to come within striking distance of victory. Semple won on the fourth ballot. After this unpropitious beginning, Lincoln moved that a principal clerk be picked, and another veteran, David Prickett, was the unanimous choice. Another clerk was selected, then the office of doorkeeper was acted upon, with fourteen candidates presented. Three ballots accomplished nothing, and the House adjourned to make room for the internal improvements convention.

This convention, made up of internal improvements delegates chosen at county mass meetings, assembled to bring pressure on the legislature, and was so large that only the House chamber would hold it. Subsequently described by the House internal improvements committee as "highly talented and respectable . . . , composed of delegates fresh from the people, and convened under circumstances of privation, which argued much for their patriotism and devotion to the country," the convention occupied the seats of House members on the first three afternoons of the session. The delegates agreed on the need for internal improvements. But debate arose over how best to get them done, one group wanting the state to make all improvements, the other demanding that government merely assist chartered corporations. A compromise was reached, which recommended improvement of principal rivers only, a north-south and an east-west railroad, and state assistance for companies engaged "in constructing other works of a less general nature." Both Vandalia papers declined to publish news of the convention, rightly guessing that the movement might work against Vandalia's capital interests. But the adopted resolutions easily found their way into legislative hands.[24]

Tuesday morning the House picked a doorkeeper in two more ballots. Preliminary organization completed, the members fled the clammy chamber and warmed themselves in taverns nearby. Nothing was done Wednesday beyond adopting the rules of the last session, with minor changes, and on Thursday the House met only long enough to adjourn. Friday morning's session lasted five minutes. Many of the more interested and less thirsty members spent their free time watching a battle in the Senate across the hall. Lieutenant Governor Jenkins had resigned to become president of the new Illinois

Central Railroad Company, and a presiding officer had to be chosen before the Senate was ready for legislative business. Democratic schism was revealed in full light, and a Whig, William H. Davidson of White County, was chosen president *pro tempore* after a three-day struggle.

Friday afternoon the Senate gave notice that they had organized, and were ready for the governor's message, which was long and full of dynamite. Few members remained to hear the clerk read it through; damp plaster made the room uncomfortable, and they could read it in print. The United States was at peace, affirmed the governor, and prosperous. So was the state. Health was excellent. Finances were also in good shape. He asked the legislature to take steps to receive Illinois' share of "the surplus revenue of the United States," and to place the money in an internal improvement fund. On the important subject of improvements, declared Duncan, his views "have underwent [*sic*] no change." He urged:

> . . . a general law providing that the State take a certain amount of the capital stock in all canals and rail-roads, which may be authorized by law, wherever private individuals shall take the remainder. . . . Under such policy I have no doubt that many works of great value to the community would be immediately commenced, and carried into effect, which, if left to individual enterprize, unaided, would remain untouched for years to come.
>
> Should the State be true to her own interest, and take one half, or one third, of the stock in all works of internal improvements, she will hasten the completion of the most important first, and secure to herself a lasting and abundant revenue . . . , until the whole country shall be intersected by canals and rail-roads, and our beautiful prairies enlivened by thousands of steam engines, drawing after them lengthened trains freighted with the abundant productions of our fertile soil.[25]

The governor hoped the legislature would promptly pay for the new capitol building, indited an essay on the virtues of education, reported slight progress on the Illinois and Michigan Canal, and expressed his confidence in the state bank. Then he delivered an assault on President Jackson. The "Hero

of New Orleans" was declared guilty of violating the Constitution, and of nepotism, autocracy, perversion of the principles
of office-holding, extravagance, and other practices menacing
to free government. These customs must not be allowed to become precedents. The legislatures of the states must face them
"fearlessly and frown them down."

The message was laid on the table and 3,000 copies ordered
printed. Democrats were enraged. But John Dement was not
too angry to present a resolution (adopted) calling for a joint
committee to investigate the new capitol and provide for payment if they found the new building justified.

With little business to discuss during the first week-end of the
session, members and interested observers concentrated on
Duncan's diatribe and the impending selection of a United
States Senator. Barroom and corridor opinion held that two
judges, Richard M. Young and Samuel McRoberts, were the
only candidates who had a chance. Whigs preferred Young,
for McRoberts had "always gone with the administration,
right or wrong." [26]

Standing committees were named Saturday morning. Lincoln's prominence caused him to be put on two committees,
the important one on finance and the unimportant penitentiary committee. His six Sangamon colleagues were appointed
to one committee each. Dawson, recently chairman of the
committee on internal improvements, was reappointed, but
not as chairman. Douglass, though a first-termer, was named
chairman of the important, overworked committee on petitions. These appointments settled, the members did not linger.
"The plaster is new and damp," admitted the Vandalia
Register, "and it became necessary to the comfort and health
of the members to have additional stoves put up. The workmen
have been engaged with unwearied industry in finishing the
rooms and putting up the stoves." [27]

Before departure, a number of quick motions were heard,
chiefly on internal improvements. Duncan's recommenda-
tions were spurned. Had not private improvements been tried

already, by those corporations chartered at the recent special session, and with what result? Not an inch of track had been laid, not a spadeful of dirt turned. Dawson, paying no attention to the governor's scheme, asked "That the committee on Internal Improvements be instructed to inquire into the expediency of creating a loan of —— millions of dollars, by pledging the faith of the State for payment of said loan to aid said State in carrying out a system of internal improvement." Nothing came of this, for on Wednesday of the second week, after two more days of waiting for the plaster to dry, Douglass took the initiative. This was satisfactory to the Sangamon delegation; the issue was thus made non-partisan. He introduced a resolution calling upon the internal improvements committee to report a bill providing for the Chicago canal, a north-south and an east-west railroad, river improvements, and "for surveys and estimates of such other works as may be considered of general utility." [28] All improvements were to be state owned and constructed, and financed by a loan. This proposal was referred to the committee of the whole House, and made the order of the day for the following Monday.

Lincoln and his followers now bestirred themselves. On Tuesday, December 13, when the House met for one minute, Lincoln had little to do, and wrote a personal letter to Miss Mary Owens, toward whom he entertained indecisive matrimonial ambitions. Working in the damp capitol had given him a cold. He began:

> I have been sick ever since my arrival. . . . The new State House is not yet finished, and consequently the legislature is doing little or nothing. The Governor delivered an inflamatory political Message, and it is expected there will be some sparring between the parties about it as soon as the two Houses get to bussiness. . . .
>
> Our chance to [take the] seat of Government to Springfield is better than I expected. An Internal Improvement Convention was held here since we met, which recommended a loan of several millions of dollars on the faith of the State to construct Rail Roads. Some of the legislature are for it and some against it; which has the majority I can not tell. There is great strife and

struggling for the office of U. S. Senator here at this time. It is probable we shall ease their pains in a few days. The opposition men have no candidate of their own, and consequently they smile as complacently at the angry snarls of the contending Van Buren candidates and their respective friends, as the christain [*sic*] does at Satan's rage. . . .[29]

By the next day business was moving fast behind the scenes. Internal improvements, clearly, were the wish and demand of the people. Public meetings in all parts of the state had asked for them. The legislature had but to decide on what improvements, where they would be made, and how. Here was Sangamon's opportunity. Every county wanted a railroad, or canal, or improved roads, or waterway improvements, or all of them together. Legislators, mindful of election day in 1838, were anxious to do the best they could for the folks back home. The situation was ideal for well-planned logrolling, and the Long Nine set about it, promising to vote for a railroad here, a post road there, a waterway deepened elsewhere, in return for support of Springfield as the next capital. This began at once, lest the internal improvements bill be written before their arrangements had been made. Champions of Alton and Vandalia at once tried using the same method, but they had not the strength of the Sangamon nine.[30] Affirming his ambition of becoming "the DeWitt Clinton of Illinois," Lincoln circulated among his colleagues in corridor, council chamber, and taproom, an amiable, entertaining apostle of adequate transportation for every county in the state.[31] Picking DeWitt Clinton as a model was apt, for Clinton was the New York politician behind the profitable Erie Canal, an internal improvement that was the envy of the West.

Wednesday afternoon, December 14, as Sangamon's missionary work began, the Senate joined the House to elect a United States Senator. Most of the Long Nine voted for Archibald Williams, who finished third on three ballots. The winner was Richard M. Young, independent Democrat, former representative, and circuit judge. Young's election gave Whigs some comfort, for he defeated, with Whig assistance, Judge McRoberts of the Supreme Court, a whole-hog Jacksonian. Young's victory evoked a banquet of celebration at one of the public houses. Food and refreshments were the best available. The customary supper of wild game, which the solons encountered so often that they hated the sight of cooked duck and wild turkey, gave way to civilized fare. Douglass and Shields, having generously sampled the liquid refreshments, astonished the assemblage by climbing on the loaded table and executing a lively dance. The crowd roared as the two uninhibited Democrats pirouetted the length of the table through clouds of smoke, singing, shouting ribaldries, sending dishes and goblets in every direction. At the end of an allnight spree the landlord billed Judge Young six hundred dollars for supplies and breakage. "This is now a Terrible place," wrote a visiting minister. "Greate Room for Reforme." Observations at the capital convinced him that church members did not pay enough attention to elections. Something ought to be done about it.[32]

With the senatorial election out of the way, wrote the *Sangamo Journal's* Vandalia correspondent,

> . . . the bustle, whisperings and fence-corner privacies ceased, and a true spirit of business seemed to prevail in each branch of the assembly—committees . . . went quietly to work in right earnest, notwithstanding the frequent pulls of the sleeve and beckonings in the street, to which they were subject, by would-be circuit judges and attorneys.

Monday afternoon, December 19, as scheduled, the House metamorphosed itself into a large committee and discussed the Douglass internal improvement program. A long debate made it clear that a moderate schedule of improvements, such as recommended by the convention, would not be approved. As the legislature actually began work both houses were flooded with memorials praying establishment of railroads, bridges, canals, turnpikes; and more were to come. These regularly went to internal improvements committees of both houses, to whom fell the task of pressing the manifold appeals into a bill and enacting it. Clearly nothing short of a program imperial in its proportions would satisfy the voters.[33]

Opponents of lavish expenditures labored along two lines to stem the tide. Were Illinois voters, after years of watching every penny, prepared to spend millions? This was not necessary, proponents of improvements replied as they painted a roseate picture of canals and railroads paying for themselves and, ere long, even returning annual operating profits to the treasury. The Erie Canal had done so, and Illinois projects could do likewise. But there were legislators who did not believe railroads and canals could be built for nothing, and they attempted early to interest the legislature in a general land tax law.[34] In addition, reprisals were undertaken against the two largest delegations, Morgan and Sangamon. Morgan County favored capital relocation because Jacksonville might be chosen, and was strong for internal improvements as a means to that end. If the two big counties could be cut down, the strong and ambitious delegations from Morgan and Sangamon would perceptibly suffer. A bill marking off a new county from Morgan and Sangamon appeared on the calendar at the end of the second week.

This was embarrassing to the Long Nine, and doubly so to Lincoln. Sangamon County, twice the size of Rhode Island, was too large for the convenience of citizens living far from Springfield. Residents around New Salem had been trying since 1830 to induce the legislature to create a new county in the northwestern part of Sangamon. John Taylor of Springfield, internal improvements convention delegate, land speculator, receiver of the land office, and promoter of Petersburg, hard by New Salem, appeared in Vandalia with a formidable petition asking a new county. If this were ignored, Lincoln might be defeated in 1838, and so might others of the Long Nine. But if the Sangamon delegation were to put through the new county, a delegation of seven representatives would shrink, in 1838, to five or less. Lincoln's course was cautious and astute. Taylor gave the dangerous petition to McCormick for introduction. The Long Nine revised it; the prayer now asked that part of Morgan County be lopped off also, thus insuring the opposition of members from Morgan. McCormick presented the doctored petition December 15. Dawson moved to lay it on the table but lost, and the petition went to Douglass' committee on petitions. Dawson then presented a remonstrance, which went to the same committee.[35]

Ordinarily, the next step would have been a great coming and going of envoys between Springfield and Vandalia. But the capital was completely cut off by bad roads, and communication with Springfield was impossible until after Christmas. A sudden freeze and heavy snow followed days of steady rain. Before travel was restored the division bill had been successfully dealt with. Douglass' committee reported, December 20, that signers of the division petition outnumbered signers of the remonstrance, that Morgan County petitioners totaled "a very small number." Therefore the prayer for a new county affected Sangamon only. Petitioners appeared to comprise a majority of Sangamon voters. "Anxious to conform," said Douglass, "as near as possible to the wishes of a majority of the citizens of Sangamon county, a majority of the committee have directed me to report a bill for the establishment of a new county." The Long Nine had no member on the Douglass committee, but they had not been idle while the petition was being discussed there. Some of them had appeared in person at its meetings. Douglass concluded, "for the purpose of avoiding all difficulties that might possibly arise, they have inserted a provision referring it to the voters of Sangamon county for their approval or disapproval." This seemed satisfactory. A referendum would stave off division until 1839. But that provision might have been put in as strategy, to be removed before passage. To make sure, Lincoln moved that the bill be referred to a select committee, and was made its chairman.

When the House was called to order the next morning, December 21, Lincoln obtained the floor and moved that a minority report of the petitions committee, made by Robert Stuart of Tazewell, which opposed division of Sangamon County, "be spread upon the Journal." Lincoln was the real author of this minority report. It denied that the petition carried signatures of a legal majority, reminded the House that the petition called for a new county in Sangamon *and* Morgan, and hinted that "private speculation" was the motive for division. Stuart had not been able to present his dissent. The Speaker was not sure how to handle it. But Semple investigated the question of minority reports that night, in Jefferson's *Manual* of legislative procedure, and concluded they had no standing. Congress, however, generally printed minority along with majority reports, and a motion might therefore be entertained to print it as a protest. Lincoln so moved. Linder of Coles, the orator, objected. Needless printing expense, he declared. There were other ways in which the gentleman from Sangamon could put the report before his constituents.

Lincoln replied in kind. He thought he knew as much about the rights of Sangamon citizens as did someone not their representative. He also thought it "uncourteous, and a departure from the rules of etiquette, for the gentleman from Coles to meddle in the matter at all." Linder's real objective, hinted the aroused speaker, was not to save printing but to injure Sangamon County.

Debate thundered on. No, said Linder, he intended no injury, and he knew as much about courtesy as some others he could mention. If Sangamon wanted the minority report printed, let them do it "out of their own pockets. They are rich enough, God knows; they hold the bag, like Judas" — an allusion to the state bank at Springfield, object of Linder's intense dislike. "Mr. Speaker," he went on, "I have but little love for Sangamo. It has as little claim upon the generosity of the Democracy of this state, as any portion of God's heritage," having gone Whig. How would the House benefit by printing the report? But Lincoln wanted it to go home to his constituents. The *House Journal*, pointed out Linder in tones of disgust, could not reach them for months. "Mr. Speaker," he declaimed, driving home his point, "I would advise the gentleman to move for the printing of 3,000 copies of this report for the especial benefit of his constituents! Will not you gentlemen of the House, go to the expense of printing 3,000 copies for the benefit of Sangamo? But before you do, consider awhile whether your constituents may not teach you another sort of courtesy."

Bested, Lincoln managed to reply "that it was marvelous what talents some gentlemen possessed, and how determined they were that the House and the world should have the benefit of them." Lincoln's motion to print was then voted down, 44 to 24. He sent the report to Simeon Francis, the Springfield Whig editor, who printed it in the *Sangamo Journal*.[36]

An hour after his defeat at Linder's hands Lincoln reported the division bill with amendments. Further amendments were argued, Dawson, Lincoln, Stone, and Douglass participating. Lincoln frankly described the bill as a compromise; voters of Sangamon should themselves be allowed to decide. All the next day the House debated the bill. Linder tried to amend further, to remove the plebiscite provision entirely; defeated, he tried another amendment limiting the referendum to voters of the new county, to be named Van Buren, and lost again. Lincoln, Stone, Douglass, Webb, and Hardin took part, besides Linder, in an argument carried on "with great animation." As night fell the bill was referred to a second special committee, with Ninian W. Edwards as chairman. Next morning Edwards reported the bill, again amended, and it moved ahead toward passage, an event of December 24. The Long Nine had beaten down a determined attack upon their prestige and unity.[37]

These events occurred before news of them reached Springfield, thanks to bad roads. Nevertheless, in the town which intended to be capital a lively debate sprang up between divisionists and anti-divisionists, calculated to influence the

Senate. John Taylor had obtained signatures to the division petition, it was charged, by employing men to get signers at ten cents each. These employees had circulated road petitions, which everyone signed by habit, then snipped off the road petitions and attached the signatures to the division petition. Names were listed and affidavits collected. Of actual division petition signers, more than a hundred had signed twice, and many three times. "Barefaced corruption," charged Archer G. Herndon in a letter to the Whig editor. Ninian W. Edwards cried "FRAUD" in another. "Villainous proceedings have taken place TO DECEIVE THE PEOPLE." [38] But the divisionists did not give up. If northern speculative management could not succeed, identical interests in east and south might unite and fare better. Sangamon could be cut up into four counties. A new division petition was circulated. A new remonstrance, carrying an unprecedented number of signatures, was made up and taken to the capital.

Taylor retaliated, charging that signatures on the new remonstrance were obtained "on false and deceitful pretences." He insisted that a majority of Sangamon voters were for division. But to no avail. When the House bill reached the Senate, Herndon effectively killed it. The quartering petition and remonstrance came up in the House on February 9, as the battle on the omnibus internal improvements bill was about to be joined, and Lincoln made short work of it. [39]

While the House considered the division bill, matters of more general importance developed. The Senate passed a bill accepting Illinois' share of the federal surplus, but could not resist the opportunity to stab Jackson's fiscal policy. The money must be "in specie;" no other kind, the Whig Senate implied, would be worth having. This raised a storm in the Democratic House. Democrats debated the specie demand all one afternoon. It was impudent; it would require Illinois' collecting agent "to roll the specie from Washington to Illinois, in kegs;" it would cause bank failures. After the specie provision was removed by a strict party vote, the bill passed the House unanimously, and the Senate, having made its point, backed down and concurred.[40]

For two days before the Christmas recess the House got nothing accomplished beyond heated discussion of national politics from a fresh angle. Governor Duncan's strictures on Jackson had gone to a special committee of seven, all Democrats. When they reported, December 23, "a true jesuitical cant party report," in the words of the *Sangamo Journal's* Vandalia correspondent, "every thing like sober and legitimate legislation" ended for two days. "It had the effect, as no doubt was intended, to blow up the smouldering embers of party heat and violence." A long report covered the "Hero of New Orleans" with a coat of shining whitewash. The committee offered resolutions approving Jackson's administration and disavowing Duncan's charges. Hardin of Morgan moved a substitute which resolved that, since the legislature was occupied with internal improvements, education, "and other subjects of vital importance," it was not expedient to waste time and money "acting upon any resolutions which merely involve national politics." This was defeated more than two to one, and the committee resolutions were approved by votes even more one-sided, in spite of the best Whig efforts.[41]

Attendance was low around the Christmas holiday, and little legislative progress was made until the new year. The anonymous capital correspondent spent Christmas day writing two long letters to the *Sangamo Journal*. On January 7, the first Saturday of 1837, as preliminaries to the internal improvements drive were mostly out of the way and the main battle over what each county was to get seemed imminent, Linder jolted the House with another attack on Sangamon County, in the form of resolutions asking an investigation of the Illinois State Bank at Springfield. Old Theophilus W. Smith, the impeached, acquitted judge, was the brain behind this move. Smith had written the bill establishing the bank, a service for which he naturally expected favors. Getting none from the managers, Smith decided that these ingrates must be made to squirm, and while baiting them he could also strike a blow at the northerly shift of power in Illinois, which threatened the control of old southern Illinoisans like himself.

The judge boarded at a private house which had two other lodgers, Usher F. Linder and Mrs. Linder. Attracted by Linder's aggressive instincts and hostility to the Long Nine, Smith asked him one December evening if he would like to become a great man. Linder would. Very well, replied the former student of Aaron Burr, "I will put you on the high road to become such, if you will follow my advice and instructions." Smith sat down and wrote a series of resolutions calling for a bank investigation. Linder introduced them. They were long, hostile in tone, and asked that a committee of seven investigate all details of the bank's business. The Democratic House, suspicious of all banks, was interested. The resolutions were ordered printed, for careful study.

On Wednesday and Thursday afternoons of the next week the subject was vigorously debated. Linder, attacker, and Lincoln, defender, held the spotlight. Primed by Smith, who stood at his elbow, Linder made a powerful speech supporting the resolutions and attacking the bank's money practices. Lincoln, armed with facts and arguments supplied by friends of the bank who arrived posthaste from Springfield, replied with an equally powerful defense. His speech was extremely able. Published in the Vandalia Whig paper and reprinted in the *Sangamo Journal*, it was his first published address. "Our friend carries the true Kentucky rifle," remarked Simeon Francis by way of comment on the speech, "and when he fires he seldom fails of sending the shot home." Other speakers attacked Linder's resolutions, and he was finally forced to substitute a new one calling for a limited investigation only, which was adopted, then sidetracked in favor of a similar Senate resolution. Linder's anti-Sangamon eloquence had again been put down.[42]

One more problem remained in the way of the internal improvements denouement—slavery. Alarmed by abolitionist verbal violence, southern legislatures sought assurances from their northern counterparts. On December 29 Governor Duncan laid before the Vandalia lawgivers resolutions and memorials from several southern states on the subject of abolition agitation and its evils. After committee consideration, the matter came before the House on January 12, in the midst of the bank squabble. Illinois, according to the committee, deplored abolition societies, affirmed the "sacred" right of slave property under the Constitution, and declared that the national government had no right to abolish slavery in the District of Columbia without the consent of residents. Lincoln wanted to add a mild amendment implying the right of District citizens to petition for abolition, but did not press it. After moderate debate and maneuver the resolutions were adopted, 77 to 6. The six dissenters were Lincoln, McCormick, and Stone of Sangamon, Gideon Minor of Edgar, John H. Murphy of Vermilion, and Parvin Paullen of Pike.[43] Lincoln had further action in mind on the slavery resolutions, but held his peace until after more important current business, internal improvements and capital relocation, had been dispatched.

Immediately after the slavery vote on January 20, Lincoln's friend Hogan of Belleville moved that a bill entitled "An act to establish and maintain a general system of Internal Improvements" be taken from the table. It was read a second time, by title, under suspension of the rules. Hogan then moved successfully that the bill be referred to the internal improvements committee, of which he was an enthusiastic member. He wanted another look at the complex arrangements before the bill was subjected to concentrated fire of opponents and amenders. Florid, voluble John Hogan had concerned himself primarily, since arrival, with preaching the improvements gospel. The picture he painted to anyone who would listen was a broad network of enterprises financed by fifteen or twenty million borrowed dollars. Illinois bonds "would go like hot cakes." The Rothschilds and Baring Brothers would scramble for them; the price would rise from fifty to a hundred percent above par. This premium alone would pay for most of the works; the principal would go into the treasury and make taxes unnecessary for years.[44] While these extreme views were exceptional, only a few legislators doubted that the idea would work out on a smaller scale.

The House internal improvements committee, after absorbing scores of petitions and resolutions for three weeks, had reported on January 9. Four thousand copies of the report, with an accompanying bill, were printed. The committee, admitting its views to be "limited and imperfect," was positive that a general program must be undertaken. On all sides sister states were "adopting and prosecuting gigantic schemes of improvement," and "the patriot and enlightened statesman of Illinois" must decide "whether he will sit still and witness his adopted State sleeping over all her means of wealth, social comforts and happiness; or whether he will step forward in the support of a system of Internal Improvements, and by his energies and example, calm the apprehensions of the timorous, and oppose the attack of calculating opposers." Immigration would slow down and population would decline, if Illinois did not improve. A loan of eight millions was proposed. Choosing the works to be improved "from amongst the variety, which . . . were presented to your committee by honorable members, formed one of the most delicate and embarrassing" of the committee's duties. They had decided on a general, rather than a universal schedule, to cost approximately seven and a half millions: seven millions for one north-south and two east-west railroads; a hundred thousand for road improvements; and four hundred thousand for improvement of five rivers.[45] This was the Douglass program, somewhat altered.

Pressure was immediately exerted to enlarge the schedule. One lobby orator proclaimed that a hundred million would not be too much to borrow and spend. Meeting nightly in the capitol, as usual, the lobby held lively sessions attended by large numbers of interested parties. So many appeared each evening to argue by candlelight that a full unofficial roster of officers had to be chosen to expedite business. The fabulous "Lord Coke," president, published the list of officers in the Vandalia *Free Press*, describing Theophilus Washington Smith as a leading light in terms which aroused the noted Smith temper. Confronted with a demand for satisfaction, the ragged "Lord" hastily declared that he had not written the paragraph which offended the bellicose jurist.[46]

The improvements bill went back to committee January 20, and amendments were considered. This meant hard work for the Long Nine. Counties left out must somehow be included, so that the grateful beneficiaries would vote for Springfield as the next capital. "Our Correspondent" could not find time to report legislative progress to the *Sangamo Journal*. After a hard week-end of laborious amending, the bill was returned to the House Monday morning, January 23, and energetically debated for two days.

The amended bill showed the results of intensive pressure. Access to the committee was simple for the Long Nine; Dawson was the leading minority member. Lincoln spent so much time with the committee that Robert L. Wilson, thirty years later, erroneously remembered him as a member. The bill now provided ten millions for improvements. The three trunk railroads became two (Cairo to Galena; and Northern Cross, connecting Jacksonville and Danville *via* Springfield), plus six spurs connecting with the Cairo-to-Galena line. Road appropriations more than doubled, while for unfortunate counties getting neither railroad, river improvements, nor canal there was a grab-bag fund of two hundred thousand for roads. The Chicago canal, already provided for by laws of the Ninth General Assembly, was not included. Crippling amendments were moved in the House and voted down by heavy majorities as Dement bobbed up and sat down again like a diminutive jack-in-the-box. A series of amendments further increasing expenditures were also defeated. Logrolling with abandon, Sangamon's seven representatives voted together steadily in favor of a still wider program, gathering new friends by supporting expansive amendments which were not approved. A week later, on third reading, two afternoons were spent voting down amendments, and on January 31 the bill was passed, 61 to 25.[47]

The bill passed the Senate on Washington's birthday, giving double cause for celebration. The swarm of lobbyists congratulated one another with such spirit that Vandalia residents caught the enthusiasm and joined in the jollification. That evening "the huzzas and acclamations of the people were unprecedented. All Vandalia was illuminated. Bonfires were built, and fire balls were thrown, in every direction." [48] Even the Democratic *Register*, by dint of calling the law a Van Buren measure, waxed enthusiastic:

> Since the passage of the bill, the Land office here has been literally crowded with persons desirous to enter and occupy public land. We have no doubt that the passage of the bill has already increased the value of the land in the State more than 100 per cent, and every day is adding to its value. We have the utmost confidence that every acre of the public land will, in a few years, be settled by emigrants, who will add to the population of the State, will increase its wealth, its influence and power among the other States of the confederacy. If the present Legislature had done no more, they would have deserved the thanks of the People for the passage of this law.[49]

While the improvements bill was progressing through the House, the Wolf bill, providing a fifty-cent bounty for wolf "scalps with the ears thereon," established itself as a vehicle of humorous oratory. The lawmakers sensed the inappropriateness of wolf bounty discussions in a state thought to be on the threshold of greatness. One day in late January William Lane of Greene County spoke against the bill. A wolf scalp was not, said he, worth a half dollar. Peter Green of Clay County replied. He was for the bill. Painting a picture of gory nocturnal destruction by fiendish, slinking lupine "varmints," Green said he would gladly pay five dollars per scalp. Mr. Lane of Greene rose to reply to Mr. Green of Clay. "Why is it, Sir," he addressed the Speaker, "that the gentleman from Clay has been found advocating this bill, and myself opposing it?"

> Simply, Sir, because my county is densely populated with human beings and his with wolves. . . .
>
> Sir, I have not . . . the honor of representing so many prairie wolves upon this floor, as has the gentleman from Clay, and should things remain as they are, this bill would create no sources of revenue to my people. But, Mr. Speaker, there is another proposition before this honorable body, which if carried into effect, will produce a great change. . . . I have reference sir, to the stupendous and gigantic system of Internal Improvement proposed by the bill now pending in this House, and so ably advocated by that gentleman. Sir, that bill provides for the construction of a number of rail roads through the thinly settled section of country in which the gentleman resides, while the county of Greene and the country thereabouts are entirely overlooked. . . . When those roads go into operation, when the long trains of cars, laden with all sorts of *notions*, and drawn by the mighty power of steam are seen daily running thro' the dense settlements of wolves represented on this floor by the gentleman, . . . those settlements [will] be broken up. . . . The wolves will inevitably be scared away. They now roam abroad unmolested, the sole occupants of the best portions of the gentleman's county, and when they lie down to rest after the close of their daily or rather nocturnal toils, they fear no intrusions upon their repose. . . . But the days of their quiet are numbered. The fiat has gone forth, and they are to be driven from their Eden of repose. When operations are commenced on these rail roads, . . . the puffing of the engines, the clattering of the wheels, and the ringing of the 35 lb. bells, will be mighty certain to force these voracious animals to break for "high timber." I tell you, Sir, they cannot stand the racket. They will leave Clay county, and seek refuge in Greene, where the friends of the mammoth bill have taken special care that the puffing of steam engines shall not annoy them, as it is almost the only county unprovided with one or more rail roads, and the consequence will be, Sir, that my constituents will be able to make money by wolf scalps. Under these considerations, I am almost tempted to take the bounty and vote for the bill.[50]

Refreshed, the House passed the "wolf bill" amid laughter.

The passage of internal improvements cleared the track for capital relocation, a battle far more difficult. First a bill must

be passed moving the capital from Vandalia; then the legislature would meet in joint session and vote on a new location.
Long Nine strategy determined to start the relocation bill in
the Whig Senate, for the House passed Senate bills more
readily than new ones. It reached the House without difficulty
February 8, and was discussed three days later. During the
ten-day interval between internal improvements and relocation battles Lincoln was often absent from the House, working
on political fences, serving on two special committees, and
struggling with figures as a finance committee member. In
the latter capacity he managed to broaden his influence by reporting on February 10 a committee road bill which pleased
several members. To Vandalia from Springfield had come for
the final drive, charged an opponent, "the president and
directors of the State Bank . . . , [who] with the aid of the
United States land officers from Springfield, were touching
every interest and every cord that could secure a vote for their
town." [51]

The next afternoon "An act to permanently locate the seat
of Government of the State of Illinois" became House business.
Opponents, led by John Dement, employed the usual ob-
structive weapons, without success. Lincoln, in contrast to his
quiet conduct during internal improvements discussions on the
floor of the House, played an active rôle in pushing the bill
past first and second readings. Four days later the bill came up
for third reading. Fortune at first seemed to smile. Linder of
Coles resigned. Elected attorney general on January 16 — an
honor he attributed to oratorical brilliance — Linder remained
an active House member for three weeks, apparently determined to resist Springfield to the end. But his seat was vacant
February 14. Even so, difficulties arose. A move of Dement to
table the bill until December, 1839, was defeated by the
narrow margin of 42 to 38. An afternoon of debate failed to
surmount the third reading.[52]

Another afternoon of argument, three days later, was still
worse. An amendment requiring the new capital to raise fifty

thousand dollars and donate it to the state, matching a sum appropriated by the removal bill, was accepted. Sundry crippling amendments were defeated. The hour grew late and candles were lit. Members gazing idly out of the windows saw the panes heavily crosshatched by driving snow. A few at once left the hall, emerging into a violent storm. Suddenly a move to table the bill until July 4 was made, and sustained 39 to 38, with all seven Sangamon members present and voting Nay. This usually meant the end, but Lincoln did not give up. He called his six colleagues into conference at his lodgings, and gave each an assignment.[53] They went out into pelting snow to spend the night persuading five tablers to vote next morning to take the bill off the table, and urging absentees who favored relocation to disregard the weather and be in the House to vote. Thomas Atwater of Putnam, Thomas Hunt of Edwards, Edward Smith of Wabash, and Francis Voris of Peoria were sought out and pointedly asked if they had no gratitude for the railroad which ran (on legislative documents) through their respective constituencies. It was pointed out to Benjamin Enloe of Johnson that a railroad, the longest in the state, ran virtually along the western boundary of his county. Had he no gratefulness in his soul? Threats were employed. The internal improvement bill was not yet through the Whig Senate. Perhaps the Sangamon seven might be obliged to ask their Senate colleagues to erase some of those railways. Enloe agreed to move that the bill be taken up. The opposition, seeing the Long Nine in action, prevailed upon some of those who had voted against tabling, to vote the next morning to keep the bill on the table.

Saturday morning, February 18, Enloe of Johnson moved that the bill be taken off the table. Douglass demanded a roll call: affirmative 42, negative 40. A shift of one member from Yea to Nay would have left the bill on the table. Lincoln needed all his friends and influence to revive it. A countermove to table again failed by a nine-vote margin. The amending game was resumed. Fearful that his margin of victory would collapse, Lincoln moved that the bill be tabled until Monday. He left the House to plan a week-end of strategy, returning in mid-afternoon while three of his Sangamon associates departed to build fences.

The relocation bill did not come up again until Tuesday afternoon, when renewed amending attacks were defeated by comfortable margins. Lincoln's persuasive representations and threats of Senate reprisals had been effective. "Shall the bill be read a third time?" intoned Speaker Semple at dusk. Every Sangamon representative was in his place. The House voted affirmatively, 48 to 34.

Third reading came Friday afternoon, February 24. Only Dement was still moving amendments of a crippling variety. Two minor amendments were moved, accepted by Lincoln; and then he moved one of his own. This looked like a concession but was really meaningless: "The General Assembly reserves the right to repeal this act at any time hereafter." Then the bill was passed, 46 to 37.[54] The Long Nine were not yet ready to celebrate. Their work was only two-thirds done until Springfield was actually chosen as the new capital, and now there were evening sessions to attend. A hundred minor bills remained to be dealt with, and a few major ones.

The improvements act required more attention next day. The Council of Revision disapproved it, chiefly for technical reasons. Governor Duncan was against it in principle. Instead of using the usual method of overriding the veto, which the House could easily have done, the lawmakers chose the more cautious method of quickly amending the bill to meet the objections, and the Council then approved it. Council approval of the capital relocation bill reached the House Monday evening, and members agreed to admit the Senate the next morning and select the site. There was little time for strategy planning and execution; the House sat until after midnight, discussing the general appropriation bill for 1837 and '38.

The first thing next morning John Taylor, the speculator, was heard from. Newton Cloud, acting Speaker (Semple hav-

ing been absent because of severe illness since the day before—
a stroke of luck for the Lincoln cause), presented a communication from E. C. Blankenship, enclosing a memorial from himself and John Taylor offering the paper town of Illiopolis,
in eastern Sangamon County, to the state as a capital site.
The House was not interested, Lincoln having done his work
well.

The Senate marched in and roll was called. On the first
ballot the voting was chiefly geographical. Fully half the members voted to give the capital to the folks back home. Springfield ran far ahead of the field with 35; Vandalia 16; Peoria 16;
Alton 15; Jacksonville 14. Decatur had 4; five towns received
3 or 2 votes; and nine could do no better than one vote each.
Of Springfield's 35 votes, 23 were cast chiefly for reasons of
geography, 9 because the counties involved were to get a railroad, and only 3 for other reasons. Dubois and Webb were
neither close to Springfield nor in possession of a paper railroad, but they voted for Lincoln's choice. William H. Davidson of White County, Whig president *pro tempore* of the Senate,
chose Springfield for political reasons. Alton and Vandalia,
strong competitors in the 1834 election, were entirely de-
pendent on the motive of geographical proximity. The power
of internal improvement bargains was thus demonstrated on
the first ballot, indicating that a Springfield victory was only a
matter of time.

On the second ballot Springfield gained nine votes and
reached 44 (incorrectly announced as 43), every accession
coming from a railroad district at the expense of Alton, Peoria,
Decatur, and Jacksonville. Lincoln had not neglected members who, unable to help him on the first ballot, could on the
next. This gain was the only important change on ballot two.
The third vote saw Springfield gain nine more, reaching 53.
Five of these accessions came from railroad considerations,
four from votes set free by the decline of frivolous candidates.
Henry Mills of Edwards County, veteran senator, disgustedly
cast one vote for Purgatory, a place not found on the Illinois

map. Ballot four was the last, for the trend continued, Springfield gaining twenty votes for a total of 73, a strong majority.
Only the supporters of Vandalia held together on the fourth
division, and they were never a serious threat. The Long Nine
dominated the situation throughout, forming a solid center of
Springfield strength, with accretions certain as member after
member paid off a legislative debt.[55]

On the eve of victory the efficacy of Lincoln's arrangements
was not realized even by high officials. Justice Lockwood of the
Supreme Court told a relative about passage of the relocation
law:

> The law requires that both [houses] shall meet together on
> Tuesday next & vote for a place to be the future seat of govern-
> ment — Our Springfield friends are in high spirits that their town
> will be successful — I think Jacksonville stands no chance — & the
> probability is in favor of Springfield — It is however possible that
> no place will be selected & in that event it will remain here, until
> further Legislative action.[56]

Springfield's victory was a great personal triumph for
Lincoln, proof of his capacities for leadership, and also a considerable surprise. Vandalia consoled itself with the thought
that the law would be repealed next session, and forthwith began to lavish insults on the choice of the legislature:

> *How to populate a town!* — Let the roads be so bad . . . that,
> if a stranger succeeds in *getting in* . . . , he will abandon any
> notion of *getting out!*
> *Directions.* — In locating the town, select a large wet prairie or
> field, full of bogs and springs; so much so, that it will bear to be
> called Swamp-field, *Spring-field*, or the like.

Lots in Springfield had gone so high, said the Vandalia *Register*,
that nobody would buy them. If the legislature were to repeal
the relocation act, prices would come down and sales of
Springfield real estate would increase.[57]

In the future capital, the news which sounded too good to be
true was soberly reported. While the result was "hailed . . .
with universal enthusiasm," the victory was described, with
an eye to future sessions, not as an example of astute political

management, but as an instance of the legislature deciding the question "with exclusive reference to the interests of the State, and the convenience of its citizens. . . . We cannot but exult that the Representatives of the people have been just enough to determine the question on its merits." Justice, merit, wisdom—such motives were surely more permanent than political bargains.[58]

The victorious Long Nine immediately staged, at Ebenezer Capps' tavern near the state house, a celebration to which the entire legislature was invited. Most of the members came and partook generously of free champagne, cigars, oysters, almonds, raisins. Eighty-one bottles of champagne were tossed off, an imposing quantity for a legislature now numbering a hundred and ten effectives. But a good many non-members attended also. The bill, paid by Ninian W. Edwards, came to $223.50.

The lawmakers had already been in Vandalia longer than usual, and they remained one more week. Unfinished business was wound up as quickly as possible. Evening sessions became standard. Attendance was low; some had gone home already. Others remained in town for relaxation after the strain of legislative labor, and were seen on the floor only when important elections were held, such as those for internal improvements commissioners, Canal Board members, and judicial officers. A final triumph went to the Long Nine. A late bill required the state government to take a hundred thousand dollars' worth of stock in the state bank at Springfield.[59]

During this week, his constructive work safely out of the way, Lincoln drafted a statement on the slavery issue. He protested the position officially taken by Illinois, had it read in the House and printed in the *House Journal*, March 3, 1837. He could find only one supporter, Dan Stone. Lincoln and Stone believed slavery "founded on both injustice and bad policy," but thought abolition agitation tended "rather to increase than to abate its evils." They believed further that Congress had no power to interfere with slavery in the states, but did

have power "to abolish slavery in the District of Columbia." [60]
This protest aroused no public interest whatever.

When final adjournment was voted Monday morning,
March 6, nearly four hundred bills having been enacted, the
Sangamon delegation boarded the next stage north and
entered Springfield in triumph. Lincoln went on to New
Salem, but only to prepare to move to Springfield, the future
capital, where he was the current political hero. A full-fledged
lawyer since his name was enrolled by the clerk of the Supreme
Court in Vandalia, March 1, 1837, he now became the partner
of John T. Stuart. The *Sangamo Journal* of April 15 notified the
public that "J. T. Stuart and A. Lincoln, Attorneys and
Counsellors at Law, will practice, conjointly, in the courts of
this Judicial Circuit.—Office No. 4 Hoffman's Row, up
stairs."

Springfield swiftly worked out the preliminaries for receiving
the state government. The $50,000 donation was pledged by
leading citizens, and one of them, Dr. Anson G. Henry, conveyed the bond of pledge to Vandalia. Dr. Henry went armed
with a letter from Lincoln to Levi Davis, auditor. On de-
livering the bond, wrote Lincoln, Henry was to collect a small
sum from the treasurer, so that work on a new state house
could begin. "We have," concluded Lincoln, "generally in
this country, peace, health, and plenty, and no news." [61]

Soon, however, there was news, mostly bad. The panic of
1837 struck with astonishing force. Bank failures became general. The Illinois State Bank suspended specie payments in
May, a step which violated the charter and automatically
suspended the bank in sixty days. So Governor Duncan, early
in June, called a special session, to assemble in Vandalia on
July 10.

The capital, although under sentence of death, had found
merchants disinclined to move out. The legislature, spender of
millions, had paid for the new Vandalia state house, and au-

thorized "A. & H. Lee, of the town of Vandalia" to finish the
building. By summer the pride of Vandalia began to look
more like a seat of government; about the yard the debris of
construction had diminished but not disappeared. The
Cumberland Road was about to reach the Kaskaskia, and the
chief engineer employed by the internal improvements board
had been surveying the line of the central railroad from Vandalia south. Store and tavern keepers, their custom unexpectedly aided by the hot-weather session, were not at all sure
the capital would really move. Could not the removal law be
repealed at any time? The panic had exploded before actual
internal improvements could be undertaken, and those railroads by means of which removal was purchased might never
be built. The Vandalia *Register* alleged that $700 of state money
had been paid to take down the Sangamon County courthouse,
clearing a capitol site on which a foot of mud and water was
said to stand. "Why," exclaimed the outraged editor, "this
sum, paid to *take down* a house, would *build* a very good one."
Fayette County's delegation was prepared for a drive to repeal
the relocation act. John Dement had moved north, but in his
place was William L. D. Ewing, recently acting governor and
United States Senator, a man not to be discounted.[62]

The Long Nine was also changed. Stone had become a
judge; a special election had chosen for his seat young Edward
Dickinson Baker, London-born orator, self-made lawyer,
partner of Stephen Trigg Logan. A Whig, Baker had been
orator at Springfield on July 4, 1837, when the cornerstone
of the newest capitol had been laid. He could now help defend
that move. Popular, homely Archibald Williams of Quincy
could now assist his friend Lincoln as a member; he had been
elected representative from Adams County *vice* George Gal-
breath, deceased. Douglass had resigned to be register of the
land office at Springfield, but was in Vandalia to keep an eye
on developments.

While the Long Nine could look forward to making good
political use of the panic of 1837 in the elections of 1838 and

1840, the summer of 1837 promised nothing but danger. The cry of "economy" was bound to be heard again, and Springfield might not become the seat of government after all. Anxious for a session as brief as possible, not one of the Long Nine had a personal bill to introduce.

On Monday, July 10, opening day, only three of Sangamon's representatives — Dawson, Elkin, and Baker — answered roll call. Lincoln and Edwards were in their seats Tuesday morning. McCormick and Wilson of Sangamon did not arrive until Friday and Saturday, respectively, when the session was nearly half over. Governor Duncan's message, "read in part" Tuesday morning, was full of "I told you so." He blamed Jackson for the panic, recommended relief for the State Bank, and urged repeal of the internal improvements act.

A bank relief bill was put under way at once. Bank and panic, rather than repeal, were topics of paramount interest. Ewing announced his intention to introduce "An act to repeal certain laws relative to the permanent location of the seat of Government of the State of Illinois." This repealer was amended to death and finally passed by the House in a harmless form. Nor was there any disposition to repeal the improvements act. The Senate, on the contrary, moved to expedite actual construction, requiring of the board of public works a list of employees, with their salaries and duties.

The division of Sangamon County was again vainly attempted.[63] Lincoln managed to make himself sponsor (and executioner) of the division petition. A bank relief act was passed, as were dozens of local bills. Lincoln, according to his campaign promise to carry out the will of Sangamon County, introduced several such, and was a constant active participant in debate. On important matters his concern was defensive. Lest some surprise anti-Springfield move be made, he was present at every voting roll call, save one on the next to the last day.

Usher F. Linder, in Vandalia as an anti-bank lobbyist,

watched with keen interest the debate between Lincoln and
Ewing over repeal of Lincoln's masterpiece. Ewing castigated
the Long Nine, charging them with "chicanery and trickery,"
with selling out to "the internal improvement men" to obtain
the capital. Lincoln replied with such vigor that Ewing was reduced to taking a stand upon his personal record. Anyone
could see, declared the whilom colleague of Clay, Webster,
and Calhoun, that Lincoln was a statesman of no account, a
parvenu. The House declined to agree, and Linder later wrote
that he first conceived an admiration for Lincoln by watching
him defeat the redoubtable Ewing.[64]

A crowd of homeward-bound legislators reached Springfield
Sunday and Monday, and a public dinner in their honor was
quickly arranged. Begun at two o'clock Tuesday, July 25, at
Spottswood's Rural Hotel, it lasted all afternoon. "Some sixty
or seventy gentlemen" drank off upwards of forty toasts.
O. H. Browning, the speaker of longest wind, said he had supported Springfield in the best interests of the state. But victory
was really due, he declared, to the Sangamon delegation, to
"their judicious management, their ability, their gentlemanly
deportment, . . . their constant and untiring labor." A. Lincoln modestly toasted "All our friends.—They are too numerous to be now named individually, while there is no one of
them who is not too dear to be forgotten or neglected." [65]

On the Springfield public square, now state property, piles
of stone accumulated and the new capitol slowly took shape.
A few steps distant the partners of the firm of Stuart & Lincoln
busily practiced law and politics. On February 24, 1838,
Lincoln announced that he would run for re-election. Stuart
was ready to try for Congress again, and this time he would be
successful. Active campaigning began with warm weather.

On August 6 Lincoln received the highest vote of sixteen
candidates. The Long Nine, second edition, was returned in-
tact, with one exception. Robert L. Wilson of Athens, realiz-

ing that his course on Sangamon County division was unpopular in his vicinity, did not run. Elected in his place was a Democrat, John Calhoun, former surveyor, ally of John Taylor in the 1834–35 fight to divide Sangamon, who finished fourth. Archer G. Herndon was opposed for the Senate by Bowling Green of the New Salem area, a close friend of Lincoln and a vigorous divisionist. Herndon barely defeated Green. Division was the chief issue of the campaign in Sangamon, and the election result was a moderate rebuff of the Long Nine's anti-division position. No matter. They were now prepared to divide the county, for their legislative strength would not be reduced until 1840, by which time the capital would be firmly located at Springfield.

The regular session of the Eleventh General Assembly, December 3, 1838 to March 4, 1839, was destined to be the last held in the community located in the wilderness two decades earlier by Thomas Cox, Samuel Whiteside, Levi Compton, and William Alexander. But Vandalia's champions had not lost faith. Ewing, re-elected, was ready to fight again, aided, as John Dement had been, by William J. Hankins, the other representative from Fayette and Effingham counties. But Springfield would be more difficult than ever to defeat. The elections of 1838 had produced striking Whig gains. Morgan County, once represented by five Democrats and one Whig, had returned four Whigs and two Democrats. With luck, the Whigs might organize the House; the membership included 39 Whigs, 38 Democrats, 1 questionable Whig, 3 questionable Democrats, 3 who called themselves "Conservatives," and 7 of unknown persuasion. The Senate was more Whig than in 1836. A Whig senator, Robert Blackwell, was elected from the district comprising Fayette, Effingham, and Clay counties.

Outwardly the capital had not suffered by Springfield's triumph. Population had climbed to the thousand mark and a bit beyond. Vandalia's reputation as an unhealthy spot, born of the Kaskaskia's swampy bottom and spread by rivals, died hard. In the spring of 1838 the river embarrassingly filled the west bottom and overflowed a mile to the east. Yet, more store and tavern keepers bought licenses to do business in 1838 than in any previous year. Physicians continued to locate in town. In the summer a corps of engineers worked, with predictions of success, at the job of making the Kaskaskia navigable. By 1840, it was predicted, the great central railroad would be running through town.[66]

Despite adverse political winds, Vandalia still fought to retain the government. New stratagems were employed. Whigs, should they gain power in 1838, charged the *Illinois State Register*, would scuttle the internal improvements program. This tactic did not work, so the relocation law was attacked as unconstitutional. Did not the Illinois constitution locate the new state's capital for twenty years? Therefore the seat could not legally be moved until 1840! A public indignation meeting was held in the state house July 7, and a committee of thirteen drew up and published a three thousand word protest. This document reviewed (somewhat erroneously) the entire history of capital location, and pointed out that if the seat were not restored to Vandalia by the 1838–39 session, it never would be.[67]

When the House assembled Monday morning, December 3, the members were no longer troubled by damp plaster and industrious workmen. Edwin B. Webb was back, as were Jesse K. Dubois, Augustus C. French, Newton Cloud, John J. Hardin, Archibald Williams, William L. D. Ewing, and a surprising number of others. For once, former members were more numerous than new ones like Jesse Wilson Gouge of Macon County, and Germanicus Kent and Gholson Kercheval of the semi-inhabited northern region, who were having their only fling at holding office. The voters, not having thrown out incumbents *en masse*, had approved the conduct of the Tenth General Assembly. This was especially remarkable, for in the

1837 appropriations act the legislators had risked public
wrath by voting themselves a one-third increase in *per diem*
salary.[68]

The Whig *Sangamo Journal*, reviewing the election results,
declared that Whigs had in the House 46 members, against 36
"loco-focos" and 9 conservatives, and would certainly elect a
Speaker. This was over-optimistic. Six members were absent
on opening day, three Whigs and three Democrats. Putting up
the first candidate for Speaker ever proposed by the party, the
Whigs picked the logical choice, Abraham Lincoln. Democrats backed Ewing. One freshman Whig, uninitiated in party
discipline, voted for Ewing, giving him a first ballot margin
of 41 votes to 38 for Lincoln. Six votes were scattered, making
four ballots necessary before Ewing eked out a majority. Whigs
again organized the Senate. Their initial defeat in the House
was not important except as a failure to use strength won at the
polls. Had they organized the House, their control would not
have been used to carry out any definite legislative program,
for the 1838–39 session dealt with routine legislation. Broad
policy had been marked out two years earlier.[69]

And marked out disastrously, said Governor Duncan in his
final message on December 4. Again he attacked the national
administration and denounced internal improvements. Two
millions had been spent to no purpose. Cassandra then gave
way to Pollyanna as the new governor, Thomas Carlin,
promised to do the legislature's bidding. A middle-aged, unim-
pressive Irishman of limited political experience, Carlin had
been dragged out of political semi-retirement as land office receiver at Quincy, to run for governor against Cyrus Edwards,
Whig, after the first Democratic choice, James W. Stephenson,
land office receiver at Galena, was alleged to have retained for
his own uses a good share of the money paid in by purchasers
of federal land. Carlin's victory had been extremely narrow.
Nation and state, said the new governor on December 7, were
prosperous. "Pecuniary embarrassments" had been overcome
"in a much shorter period than could have been expected."

Carlin made no important proposals. His address was well written and innocuous. Whigs were certain that stronger party leaders had actually composed it.

The selection of Ewing as Speaker (Semple having taken a diplomatic post) did not mean that the House was ready to adopt Ewing's views on capital relocation. The post of honor placed him on the sidelines and required Hankins of Vandalia to lead the fight against Springfield. Shortly before Christmas Hankins induced the House to adopt a resolution requiring a full report, detailing expenditures, from the Springfield state house commissioners. It was his last victory. The Springfield builders reported expenditures of less than $6,000. Springfield's donated $50,000, plus the same amount from the state, would not, it was now clear, pay the cost of the new state house, and a Senate bill appropriating $128,300 (to be borrowed through bond issue) was before the House. Hankins hoped to kill it. But efforts to amend the appropriation bill to death were beaten by margins of two to one or more.[70]

Also concluded was the Sangamon division controversy. Lincoln made this his own concern, after repelling Vandalia's attack. He wrote and brought to passage on January 21 a law creating three new counties, Menard, Logan, and Dane (later Christian), but still leaving Sangamon large and powerful.

Internal improvements also fared well. Nearly a million more was appropriated. Times were improving, and voters wanted railroads and the rest of the works. The money expended had come, not from taxes, but from school fund and federal surplus money. Few state improvement bonds had been sold, except to state banks. But the financing plan had not yet failed. The panic ruined the bond market, and no special effort had yet been made to sell in the East and in Europe. Lawmakers thought the rosy dream could yet be achieved. If not, the state, under a law just passed, was now prepared to collect a general property tax for state expenses, a measure from which legislatures had for two decades held off as from a plague. Voters sent up immediate complaints. The internal improvements system was blamed, and a change of tune was discernible in the voice of the people.[71]

In June Governor Carlin proclaimed that, as of July 4, 1839, Springfield would become the capital of Illinois. Vandalia suffered an immediate loss of population as state officers and offices moved north without delay. Wagons loaded with furniture and public papers moved off through a deluge of rain. William Walters, public printer, followed in early August with his *Illinois State Register*, leaving Vandalia with one newspaper, William Hodge's *Free Press and Illinois Whig*. "The hospitable, generous, moral, and courteous community from which we part," wrote the departing editor, "will long remain as a green spot upon our memory. Your prosperity, which is marching rapidly forward, cannot outstrip our wishes; and we are only sorry that we can no longer be the constant witness of it." [72]

Walters was regularly accused by the Whig press of loose dealings with the truth. When he wrote in his valedictory of Vandalia's prosperity marching rapidly forward, he was clearly guilty of the charge. The march was rapid in the opposite direction. Stage transportation from Springfield ceased at once. Travelers from the north could reach Vandalia, by public conveyance, only by way of Jacksonville. A Chicago editor arrived in August by riding with A. P. Field, secretary of state, as Field pursued his criminal law practice. The desolate appearance of "the old Capital" reminded this Chicago visitor of a Latin phrase — *Ilium fuit* — Troy has existed, but exists no longer. Though Vandalia did not quite deserve to have that motto "inscribed on its ruins," it did bear, "on a small scale, . . . something of a melancholy appearance of departed greatness." Population had fallen off to 600 or less. The former state house, unoccupied, looked more like a dilapidated fortress than a temple of law. Slots in the brick walls, used for scaffolding, had never been filled, and resembled small portholes placed there for defense against a

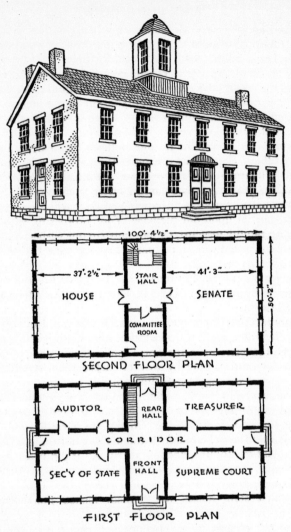

HOUSE

SENATE

STAIR HALL

COMMITTEE ROOM

100'-4½"

37'-2½"

41'-3"

50'-2"

SECOND FLOOR PLAN

AUDITOR

TREASURER

REAR HALL

CORRIDOR

SEC'Y OF STATE

SUPREME COURT

FRONT HALL

FIRST FLOOR PLAN

Third State House, 1838

marauding adversary. But the enemy had won and made off with the spoils of victory. A surrounding fence of wood was already being pulled down piecemeal for firewood.[73]

By an act of 1839 the state conveyed the new $16,000 building to the county of Fayette and the town of Vandalia, for use as a courthouse and school. Unsold land of the four sections granted to Illinois by Congress for a capital was given to the county to be sold, the money to be used for roads and bridges. Two decades later only the old capitol's outer shell of brick stood intact. Floors had been stolen, and the ruin was inhabited intermittently by "horses, cattle, mules and sheep . . . , and perhaps a few fleas and other varmints." [74]

But in 1857 the county bought out the school district and remodeled the building into one of the finest courthouses in Illinois. Large porticoes supported by massive brick pillars were built over north and south doors. In 1919 the building and grounds were purchased by the state for $60,000 for preservation as a historic memorial. Architectural restoration, begun in 1933, was completed a century after the capital moved north.

Appropriately for a place of dead hopes, the legislature in 1839 commissioned Robert Blackwell, Vandalia politician and merchant, to fence the graveyard where lay five assembly members who died "whilst absent from their families and homes, in the discharge of their official duties," and to provide tombstones. Turnover of mercantile establishments continued rapid, but on a declining scale. Partnerships gave way to single proprietors. Flack & Hogue, general store, was continued by Milton Flack as Hogue left town. William Hodge, editor of the *Free Press and Illinois Whig*, soon found that even a newspaper monopoly did not pay. He gradually withdrew from publishing and became an innkeeper, operating the Mansion House on the west side of the square. Two years later he sold the hotel and left town.[75]

The last forlorn hope, navigation of the Kaskaskia, died hard. Two prominent citizens, William C. Greenup, surveyor and speculator, and James Black, merchant, formed a navigation company in 1838. They contracted for a boat to be constructed at Cincinnati, to carry sixty tons of freight, drawing, loaded, thirty-six inches of water, and hired a boat captain. River improvements to be carried out by the state, thought

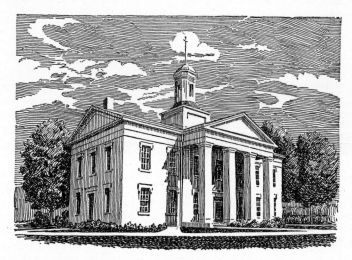

Present Restored Third State House

Colonel Greenup, indicated conclusively that the Kaskaskia could be navigated as far as Vandalia six months of the year by "steam boats drawing not more than three feet of water," and by flatboats and keelboats nine months of the year.[76] But the Kaskaskia River Navigation Company, like the railroads which took away the capital, never got into operation.

By 1850 Vandalia's population had fallen to three hundred, and the town seemed to have reached a permanent low level when the Illinois Central Railroad, from Galena to Cairo, was built through Vandalia in 1852. The town slowly recovered, elected its first mayor in 1869, and by 1900 had a population more than double that of its heyday as the seat of government.[77]

With the capital actually gone, any effort to recapture it was bound to be futile. Removal might be viewed philosophically as a work of Providence, abetted by a good deal of prodding from the Long Nine and their colleagues. The northward trend of population had been responsible for Vandalia in the first place, and the shift had not halted but accelerated, carrying away the good fortune it had brought. Nevertheless, Ewing and Hankins made a last effort when the Twelfth General Assembly met in another unfinished new capitol late in 1840. Ewing again defeated Lincoln for Speaker, this time by a wider margin. Hankins, hoping for better treatment from members elected in 1840, vainly proposed that the capital be returned to Vandalia until the state debt was paid. That would have been a long time. Uncompleted improvements were devouring state funds so rapidly that interest payments on early improvement loans came due faster than new loans could be floated to pay interest on the old.[78]

As Vandalia the victim waned, Springfield the victor waxed. Despite the collapse of internal improvements,[79] Illinois became in less than a generation a state of wealth and prominence in national councils. Its capital city prospered and crossed the threshold of fame.

The original Long Nine, engineers of these fortunes, went on to varied fates. William F. Elkin became sheriff of Sangamon County and died in 1878, in his eighty-seventh year. John Dawson's public career soon ended and, weakened by his battle wound, he died in 1850. Dan Stone, his judicial post legislated out of existence in 1841, moved back to Ohio. Robert L. Wilson moved to northern Illinois in 1840, became probate judge, toured Europe after the Civil War, and returned to write a history of Whiteside County. This he did not complete, but his work was taken over by a later historian of the county.[80] Andrew McCormick became mayor of Springfield in 1843, then retired from public life, and died in 1857. Job Fletcher's public career ended with a term in the House, 1844–46. Archer G. Herndon's was longer by virtue of his political agility. Receiving a federal appointment from the Tyler administration as receiver of public moneys at Springfield, he was able to represent himself as a lifelong Democrat so successfully that he kept the post throughout the Polk administration, losing out only when the Whigs returned to power in 1849.

On the leader of the Long Nine the weeks spent in Vandalia exerted a far more important influence. Though he was a transient resident of the west bank of the Kaskaskia for no more than forty-four weeks, only Springfield, where he lived twenty-four years, and Washington, where he spent five years as Congressman and President, exerted a larger influence. In the political struggle of the fittest, he survived and triumphed. Unknown on arrival, his political skill was apparent even to opponents when the capital moved north to Springfield. The novice had found himself, discovered the dual career of lawyer and politician, and made friends to assist him toward success in both. Confidence made him bold, facile, and clear in expression. His literary style was molded and developed in Vandalia political conflicts; the legislative custom of splitting infinitives in the titles of bills established a permanent stylistic tendency. By his statement on slavery the young lawmaker showed that he could think deeply as well as clearly, and had the courage to support a principle even against united opposition. And Lincoln learned, as perhaps his most valuable single lesson, the technique and political value of successful compromise. Throughout his public career Lincoln was to be faced, like all statesmen, by opposite forces which blocked decisive action. When he dealt with the Sangamon County division issue, compromising, taking the middle of the road, and thereby avoiding a disastrous split among his supporters, he foreshadowed his success as president in resolving the mightier conflicts between abolitionists and conservatives, on a dozen different issues of "a great civil war."

Abraham Lincoln

Re-elected to the legislature for the last time in 1840, Lincoln remained prominent in Whig affairs, went to the House of Representatives in Washington for one term, became a Republican when the Whig party expired, and achieved a national name when he debated, in 1858, with his old Vandalia opponent, Stephen A. Douglass, who had become Senator Douglas, leading Democrat of the North. An unexpected nominee for president in 1860, Lincoln won the election and was inaugurated as the sixteenth president of the United States of America.

When he lived in the Executive Mansion on Pennsylvania Avenue and dealt with complex problems of patronage, disloyalty, graft, incompetence, party control, war aims, international affairs, military strategy, only six of the Long Nine were alive. Dawson, Stone, and McCormick were dead. Fletcher and Herndon, the two senators, were old and in retirement. Of the remaining four, one was president, and he bestowed a lucrative federal appointment upon each of the remaining three. Elkin became register of the land office at Springfield; Ninian W. Edwards was appointed Captain Commissary of Subsistence; and Wilson was made a United States Army paymaster.

The Civil War president had good reason to remember his old colleagues of the House in Vandalia. They had assisted in the winning of his first political triumph. Politics and politicians were not essentially different on the Potomac and on the Kaskaskia. In Washington, as in Vandalia, he won his victory, using in his handling of national affairs a skill in practical politics which he had begun to develop three decades earlier, back in the frontier capital.

NOTES

NOTES

PART I

7   [1] Thomas Ford, *History of Illinois*, Chicago and New York, 1854, 106–107.

11   [2] *The Illinois Monthly Magazine*, II, (Jan., 1832), 172–174.

13   [3] Robert W. Ross (ed.), *Historical Souvenir of Vandalia, Illinois . . .* , Effingham, Ill., 1904, 9–11.

14   [4] *Reavis* was variously spelled *Reeves, Rivis, Reavy, Reavise, Ravis.*

14   [5] Sections 8, 9, 16, 17, township v Range 1 East of the Third Principal Meridian. "Report of Commissioners" 1st General Assembly, Illinois State Archives, Springfield, Illinois.

14   [6] John Moses, *Illinois, Historical and Statistical*, Chicago, 1889–92, I, 298; William H. Brown, "Early History of Illinois," *Fergus' Historical Series*, [Chicago, 1881], No. 14, 89.

15   [7] "List of lots sold in the town of Vandalia. . . ." Illinois State Archives.

15   [8] Ferdinand Ernst, "Travels in Illinois in 1819," *Transactions of the Illinois State Historical Society*, 1903, 163.

16   [9] F. Ernst, *Bemerkungen auf einer Reise durch das Innere der Vereinigten Staaten von Nord-Amerika im Jahr 1819*, MS. translation, Illinois State Historical Library; Charles B. Stuart, Notes on a Journey to the Western States, MS., Illinois State Historical Library, 12–13; Chester A. Loomis, *A Journey on Horseback Through the Great West in 1825*, Bath, N. Y., [182–?], 13.

16   [10] Ernst, "Travels in Illinois in 1819," *Transactions*, 150–165.

18   [11] Frederick G. Hollman, *Auto-Biography*, Platteville, Wis., [n.d.], 7–8, 11.

18   [12] Moses, *op. cit.*, I, 298.

18   [13] Daniel P. Cook to Thomas Mather, Jan. 27, 1820, Chicago Historical Society.

20   [14] Hollman, *op. cit.*, 12–13; Edwardsville *Spectator*, Dec. 26, 1820; Order Book for County Commissioners' Court, Vol. A, pp. 1, 70; John Reynolds, *My Own Times*, Belleville, Ill., 1855, 183.

20   [15] Report of Commissioners; J. D. Caton, *Address delivered on the occasion of the laying of the cornerstone of the new State House at Springfield, Ill., on Monday, Oct. 5, 1868*, Springfield, 1868.

21   [16] Moses, *op. cit.*, I, 300–306.

Page

22   [17] Thomas Lippincott's Recollections, Alton *Telegraph*, March 17, 1865.

22   [18] *Illinois Intelligencer*, Feb. 1, March 29, July 12, Aug. 9, 23, Dec. 23, 1823; *Illinois Advocate and State Register*, July 19, 1834; Hollman, *op. cit.*, 14–16.

23   [19] *Illinois Intelligencer*, Feb. 13, 1824, repeated in each issue to May 7, Nov. 12, 1824; *Laws of 1823*, 232.

23   [20] *Illinois Intelligencer*, Dec. 10, 1824.

23   [21] Ross, *op. cit.*, 21, 68–69, 168.

24   [22] Reynolds, *My Own Times*, 169.

24   [23] Ford, *History of Illinois*, 104–105; *Illinois Intelligencer*, Feb. 3, 1827.

25   [24] *Illinois Advocate*, July 19, 1834; *Illinois Intelligencer*, July 5, 1823, July 9, 1824, July 8, 1825, July 10, 1830; Edmund Flagg, *The Far West* (Early Western Travels, Vol. XXVI), I, 237.

25   [25] Ross, *op. cit.*, 35; *Illinois Intelligencer*, May 24, 1823, Jan. 9, June 4, 1824; Address of James Hall to Vandalia Antiquarian and Historical Society, 1828, in James Stuart, *Three Years in North America*, Edinburg, 1833, II, 228.

26   [26] Esther Shultz, "James Hall in Vandalia," *Journal*, Ill. State Hist. Soc., XXIII (April, 1930), 98; John T. Flanagan, *James Hall, Literary Pioneer of the Ohio Valley*, Minneapolis, [1941], 49–62; *Western Monthly Review*, Cincinnati, I, 563–565, in *Journal*, Ill. State Hist. Soc., II (Oct., 1909), 70–74; James Stuart, *Three Years in North America*, II, 227.

PART II

31   [1] *The Illinois Monthly Magazine*, II (Jan., 1832), 172–174.

31   [2] *Illinois Advocate*, Dec. 24, 1834; W. B. Archer to Jacob Harlan, Jan. 16, 1833, Harlan-Archer MSS., Illinois State Hist. Lib.; *Sangamo Journal*, April 19, 1834.

32   [3] *Illinois Advocate*, July 19, Oct. 29, 1834.

32   [4] *Ibid.*, Dec. 16, 1831, Sept. 7, 1833, Feb. 27, Nov. 19, 1834, Jan. 20, 1836; *Illinois Intelligencer*, Nov. 5, Dec. 16, 1831; *Sangamo Journal*, Jan. 10, 1835; *Illinois State Register*, Aug. 26, 1836, May 4, 1838.

33   [5] *Illinois Advocate*, Feb. 11, 18, 1835.

33   [6] John Carroll Power, *History of the Early Settlers of Sangamon County, Illinois*, Springfield, Ill., 1876, 185–186; *Illinois Advocate*, Dec. 20, 1834, Feb. 4, 1835; Ross, *op. cit.*, 26, 56.

34   [7] *Illinois Advocate*, June 3, 1831, March 16, Sept. 7, 1833, March 22, Dec. 24, 1834, Jan. 28, 31, Dec. 30, 1835.

35   [8] Beardstown *Chronicle*, Dec. 6, 1834.

35   [9] W. S. Prentice, "Recollections of Vandalia Thirty Years Ago,"
      in *History of Fayette Co.*, Philadelphia, 1878, 30.

36   [10] William Pickering to I. N. Arnold, 1866, photostat, The Abra-
      ham Lincoln Association; Daniel Roberts, "A Reminiscence
      of Stephen A. Douglas," *Harper's New Monthly Magazine*, Vol.,
      87 (Nov., 1893), 957–959; County Commissioners on March
      5, 1832, Record Book; *Illinois Advocate*, Sept. 7, 1833.

38   [11] Ford, *op. cit.*, 28, 32, 40, 103.

38   [12] *Ibid.*, 55, 89–91.

39   [13] A. D. Jones, *Illinois and the West*, Philadelphia, 1838, 101 ff.

39   [14] W. D. Howells, *Life of Abraham Lincoln* (The Abraham Lincoln
      Association edition, Springfield, Ill., 1938), 40, Lincoln's note.

40   [15] Contract between A. P. Field and Asahel Lee, 10th G. A.,
      Misc. State House Papers (misdated), Illinois State Archives;
      Illinois Intelligencer, Jan. 28, 1832; *Illinois Advocate*, Nov. 27,
      1832; *Senate Journal*, 1834–35, 412; Memorandum of Property,
      1833, made by John York Sawyer, public printer, 1832–33
      G. A., Misc. State House Accounts.

40   [16] Howells, *op. cit.*, 41. Although Douglass signed his name thus
      at this time, he dropped an *s* in later years.

42   [17] *Illinois State Register*, March 15, 1885.

42   [18] Alton *Telegraph*, Nov. 25, 1864; Usher F. Linder, *Reminiscences
      of the Early Bench and Bar of Illinois*, Chicago, 1879, 260; Quincy
      Whig, Jan. 25, 1840.

43   [19] Frank E. Stevens, "Alexander Pope Field," *Journal*, Ill. State
      Hist. Soc., IV (April, 1911), 7–37.

45   [20] For the complete list, see *House Journal*, 9th G. A., 1 sess., 3–4.

49   [21] Jones, *op. cit.*, 101 ff.

49   [22] Theodore C. Pease, *Illinois Election Returns*, Springfield, Ill.,
      1923, 268–278, lists 27 Democrats, 1 questionable Democrat,
      17 Whigs, 2 questionable Whigs, and 8 unidentified.

52   [23] Robert D. Holt, "The Political Career of William A. Richard-
      son," *Journal*, Ill. State Hist. Soc., XXVI (Oct., 1933), 226.

52   [24] Quincy *Whig*, Dec. 28, 1839.

53   [25] *House Journal*, 80, 81, 84, 86; House Bill 34, 9th G. A. MSS.,
      Illinois State Archives, copy, The Abraham Lincoln Associa-
      tion.

53   [26] *House Journal*, 103.

55   [27] *Ibid.*, 153–154; *Illinois Advocate*, Dec. 27, 1834.

56   [28] *House Journal*, 233; *Sangamo Journal*, Jan. 17, 1835.

56   [29] Douglas's speech at Ottawa, Aug. 21, 1858, in Frank E.
      Stevens, "Life of Stephen A. Douglas," *Journal*, Ill. State Hist.
      Soc., XVI (Oct., 1923–Jan., 1924), 250.

Page

57   [30] Jesse W. Fell to David Davis, Dec. 15, 1885, *Illinois State Journal*, Jan. 14, 1886.

58   [31] *House Journal*, 311, 515.

58   [32] Harry E. Pratt, *The Personal Finances of Abraham Lincoln*, Springfield, Ill., 1943, 143; *House Journal*, 343–344.

58   [33] Theodore C. Pease, *The Frontier State*, Springfield, Ill., 1918, 62–69. The major part came from taxes on lands owned by non-residents, various school funds, rent on state-owned saline lands, etc.

59   [34] *Illinois Advocate*, Dec. 24, 1834, Jan. 7, 14, 21, 31, Feb. 14, 1835; *Sangamo Journal*, Dec. 27, 1834, Jan. 10, Feb. 7, 14, 1835.

59   [35] *Sangamo Journal*, Jan. 24, 1835; *Illinois Advocate*, Dec. 17, 1834, Feb. 14, 1835.

60   [36] *House Journal*, 9th G. A., 2 sess., 404.

62   [37] Harry E. Pratt, *Lincoln, 1809–1839*, Springfield, Ill., 1941, xxxviii; MSS., 9th G. A., 1 sess., Illinois State Archives.

62   [38] Authorities on the period have not gone quite the whole distance in identifying the anonymous correspondent as Lincoln. Pratt (*Lincoln, 1809–1839*, xliii) wrote, "These letters are thought to have been written by Lincoln." A. J. Beveridge (*Abraham Lincoln*, I, 171, n. 5) concluded that the author "almost certainly was Lincoln." The style of the letters is like that of his known writings. But the strongest evidence is the fact that Lincoln was the only Sangamon County Whig continuously in the legislature during the time the letters were written, the 9th and 10th general assemblies.

62   [39] *Sangamo Journal*, Jan. 31, Feb. 7, 1835.

63   [40] "Short autobiography . . . ," June, 1860, John G. Nicolay and John Hay (eds.), *The Complete Works of Abraham Lincoln*, New York, 1905, VI, 32–33; Robert T. Lincoln Papers, Library of Congress.

64   [41] Deposition of Harvey Lee, Dec., 1836, Misc. State House Papers, 1836–37 G. A., Illinois State Archives; *House Journal*, 10th G. A., 1 sess., 840; *Senate Journal*, 334.

65   [42] *Sangamo Journal*, Feb. 6, 13, 20, 1836.

65   [43] *Ibid.*, Dec. 12, 19, 1835.

67   [44] *Ibid.*, Jan. 2, 9, 1836; the second pigeon was a convention Democrat who was defeated for the office of probate judge.

67   [45] *House Journal*, 274, 286, 305.

68   [46] *Ibid.*, 27; *Illinois Advocate*, Dec. 23, 1835, Feb. 17, 1836; Beveridge (I, 171–172) says the Senate was Whig by a majority of one. There were only 8 Whig senators (Pease, *Illinois Election Returns*, 252–255, 265–267, 279–280).

PART III

71 [1] *Illinois Advocate*, Feb. 3, March 25, 1836.

72 [2] Benjamin P. Thomas, *Lincoln's New Salem*, Springfield, Ill., 1934, 37; Pratt, *Lincoln, 1809–1839*, 52–53.

72 [3] *Sangamo Journal*, June 18, 25, July 2, 1836. The others were Dawson, McCormick, Wilson, and Edwards.

73 [4] Robert L. Wilson to William H. Herndon, Feb. 10, 1866, Herndon-Lamon MSS., Huntington Library, San Marino, Calif.

74 [5] *Sangamo Journal*, April 19, June 21, 1834.

74 [6] *Ibid.*, June 28, Sept. 27, 1834.

75 [7] Paul M. Angle, "*Here I Have Lived*," Springfield, Ill., 1935, 35–39, 54–55; *Sangamo Journal*, Nov. 19, 1836.

75 [8] *Sangamo Journal*, Nov. 26, Dec. 3, 1836.

76 [9] "Up to the Hub," in *Sangamo Journal*, July 16, 1836; Ford, *op. cit.*, 169; *Sangamo Journal*, June 25, July 16, 1836.

77 [10] Edmund Flagg, *The Far West*, New York, 1838, I, 241–245.

77 [11] *Ibid.*, I, 243–245; Store and Tavern licenses, Fayette Co. Commissioners Court Records; *Illinois State Register*, April 15, 29, Aug. 19, Dec. 2, 1836.

77 [12] Contract between Town of Vandalia and James Hankins and Abner Flack, 1836, Illinois State Archives; *Illinois State Register*, Aug. 26, Sept. 23, Nov. 18, 1836.

78 [13] Deposition of Harvey Lee, Dec., 1836, 1836–37 Miscellaneous State House Papers, Illinois State Archives; J. Duncan to A. P. Field, Levi Davis, and John Dement, Aug. 12, 1836, *ibid.*; *Illinois State Register*, Aug. 12, 1836; *House Journal*, 10th G. A., 1 sess., 479–480; *Senate Journal*, 27.

78 [14] *Illinois State Register*, Aug. 19, 1836.

78 [15] 1836–37 G. A. Misc. State House Papers, Illinois State Archives; summarized in J. F. Booton and G. M. Nedved, *Record of Restoration, Third State House, Vandalia, Ill.*, 1945, 35; *Illinois State Register*, Dec. 8, 1836.

79 [16] William Wilson to Mrs. Wilson, Dec. 29, 1836, Wilson MSS., Ill. State Hist. Lib.

80 [17] Pease, *Illinois Election Returns*, 265–267, 279–280, 283–303.

80 [18] Moses, *op. cit.*, I, 407; Charles P. Johnson, "Personal Recollections of Some of the Eminent Statesmen and Lawyers of Illinois," *Transactions*, Ill. State Hist. Soc., 1904, 28.

82 [19] Linder, *Reminiscences*, 35–41, 55–58, 65–67, 99–102, 220–224, 266–267, 371–373; Quincy *Whig*, Jan. 16, 1841; C. P. Johnson, *op. cit.*, 29–39; John F. Snyder MSS., Ill. State Hist. Lib.

83 [20] Linder, *op. cit.*, 280.

84   ²¹ J. C. Power, *op. cit.*, 244, 278–279, 281–282, 301–302, 372–373, 464, 486–487, 690, 775–776; Pease, *Illinois Election Returns, passim;* Quincy *Whig*, Dec. 28, 1839.

86   ²² Reynolds, *My Own Times*, 321; Linder, *op. cit.*, 148, 333–334, 348, 238–239.

86   ²³ *Illinois State Register*, Dec. 9, 1836.

87   ²⁴ *House Journal*, 10th G. A., 1 sess., 5–10, 204; *Illinois Patriot*, clipped in *Sangamo Journal*, Dec. 24, 1836; *Sangamo Journal*, Dec. 17, 1836.

88   ²⁵ *Senate Journal*, 10th G. A., 1 sess., 16–17.

89   ²⁶ Vandalia correspondence, Dec. 11, *Sangamo Journal*, Dec. 17, 1836.

89   ²⁷ *Illinois State Register*, Dec. 15, 1836.

90   ²⁸ "Autobiography of Stephen A. Douglas," *Journal*, Ill. State Hist. Soc., V (Oct., 1912), 341.

91   ²⁹ Lincoln to Mary Owens, Dec. 13, 1836, photostat, The Abraham Lincoln Association.

91   ³⁰ Alton's House delegation (Madison Co.) numbered three; Vandalia's (Fayette and Effingham counties) two.

91   ³¹ William H. Herndon and Jesse W. Weik, *Herndon's Life of Lincoln* (Angle ed., 1930), 140.

92   ³² *Sangamo Journal*, Dec. 17, 24, 1836; Ida M. Tarbell, *Life of Abraham Lincoln*, New York, 1900, I, 145; Benjamin Godfrey to Theron Baldwin, Jan. 5, 1837, MS., Ill. State Hist. Lib.

93   ³³ Vandalia correspondence, Dec. 25, *Sangamo Journal*, Dec. 31, 1836; *House Journal*, 59, 63, 65, 69, 79, 168–174.

93   ³⁴ *House Journal*, 29–30, 55.

94   ³⁵ Lincoln to Mary Owens, Dec. 13, 1836, *Works*, I, 17; *House Journal*, 53, 55.

96   ³⁶ *Sangamo Journal*, Dec. 17, 31, 1836, Jan. 7, 1837; Joseph Duncan to Mrs. Duncan, Dec. 18, 1836, Elizabeth Duncan Putnam, "The Life and Public Services of Joseph Duncan . . . ," *Transactions*, Ill. State Hist. Soc., 1919, 157; *House Journal*, 83; *Illinois State Register*, Jan. 12, 1837.

96   ³⁷ *House Journal*, 86, 88–89, 92–94, 123; *Illinois State Register*, Jan. 12, 1837; *Sangamo Journal*, Dec. 31, 1836, Jan. 12, 1837; M. L. Houser, *Lincoln's Early Political Education*, Peoria, Ill., 1944, 20–25.

97   ³⁸ *Sangamo Journal*, Jan. 28, Feb. 11, 1837.

97   ³⁹ *Ibid.*, Feb. 18, 25, 1837; *House Journal*, 527, 584.

98   ⁴⁰ Vandalia correspondence, Dec. 17, *Sangamo Journal*, Dec. 24, 1836.

Page

98   [41] Vandalia correspondence, Dec. 25, *Sangamo Journal*, Dec. 31, 1836; *House Journal*, 102–117.

99   [42] Linder, *op. cit.*, 260–261; *Illinois State Register*, Jan. 12, 1837; *Works*, I, 19–34; *Sangamo Journal*, Jan. 28, 1837; *House Journal*, 195–198, 236–237, 247, 288, 296–297, 302–306.

100   [43] *House Journal*, 134, 241–244, 248–249, 309–311.

101   [44] Linder, *op. cit.*, 59–60.

101   [45] *House Journal*, 202–215.

102   [46] Ford, *op. cit.*, 185; *Illinois State Register*, Feb. 16, 1837.

103   [47] Wilson to Herndon, Feb. 10, 1866, Herndon-Lamon MSS., Huntington Library; *House Journal*, 363–376, 413, 432–433, 441–443.

103   [48] *Sangamo Journal*, March 4, 1837.

103   [49] *Illinois State Register*, March 6, 1837.

104   [50] *Ibid.*, Feb. 10, 1837.

105   [51] *House Journal*, 546; *Illinois State Register*, July 20, 1838.

105   [52] *House Journal*, 592–594.

106   [53] Wilson to Herndon, Feb. 10, 1866, Herndon-Lamon MSS., Huntington Library.

107   [54] *House Journal*, 608–610, 612–614, 661–666, 701–703; *Laws of 1837*, 321–322.

109   [55] John G. Nicolay and John Hay, *Abraham Lincoln, A History*, New York, 1890, I, 138; *House Journal*, 752–759.

109   [56] Samuel D. Lockwood to Mary V. Nash, Feb. 26, 1837, copy, The Abraham Lincoln Association.

109   [57] *Illinois State Register*, May 6, 1837.

110   [58] *Sangamo Journal*, March 4, 1837; during the Eleventh General Assembly, when the House was debating whether to spend more money on internal improvements or to cut down the works in progress, Lincoln admitted that he and his Sangamon colleagues had made solemn pledges in 1836 and 1837 to support internal improvements, and intended to do so. (*Illinois State Register*, May 3, 1839)

110   [59] *Illinois State Register*, March 6, 1837.

111   [60] *House Journal*, 817–818.

111   [61] Lincoln to Levi Davis, April 19, 1837, G. A. Tracy (ed.), *Uncollected Letters of Abraham Lincoln*, Boston and New York, 1917, 2.

112   [62] *House Journal*, 840; *Illinois State Register*, May 6, June 17, 1837.

113   [63] *Illinois State Register*, July 15, Aug. 4, 1837; *House Journal*, 10th G. A., spec. sess., 21, 113, 121, 140.

114   [64] Linder, *op. cit.*, 62–63.

Page

114   65 *Sangamo Journal*, July 29, 1837.

116   66 *Illinois State Register*, March 1, June 3, 10, 29, 1837; Aug. 10,
      1838; fifteen stores in 1836, nine in 1837, twenty-six in 1838
      (County Commissioners Court Record Book).

116   67 *Illinois State Register*, July 6, Aug. 10, 1838.

117   68 A. W. Snyder to James Semple, March 21, 1837, Snyder MSS.,
      Ill. State Hist. Lib.

117   69 *Sangamo Journal*, Aug. 25, Dec. 8, 1838; *House Journal*, 11th
      G. A., 1 sess., 5–6; *Illinois State Register*, Dec. 5, 1838.

118   70 *House Journal*, 10–17, 26–30, 119, 122–123, 125–127, 137,
      140–141, 152, 181–189, 199.

119   71 *Illinois State Register*, March 22, 29, 1839; *Sangamo Journal*, April
      5, 1839.

119   72 *Illinois State Register*, Aug. 2, 1839.

121   73 Chicago *Daily American*, Aug. 7, 8, 1839.

121   74 Ross, *op. cit.*, 23.

121   75 *Free Press and Illinois Whig*, April 4, 1839, Aug. 28, 1841.

122   76 William C. Greenup to James Black, July 12, 1838, copy, The
      Abraham Lincoln Association.

123   77 Ross, *op. cit.*, 19, 23, 28.

123   78 A persistent Vandalia tradition states that Lincoln and two
      Whig colleagues, to prevent a quorum, jumped out a window
      of the House. The exact spot is exhibited with pride. This in-
      cident, however, occurred in Springfield, Dec. 5, 1840, when
      House and Senate met temporarily in two churches.

123   79 Illinois began defaulting on interest payments in 1841, but at
      the end of the decade, to restore the state's credit, payment
      was resumed, and the last of the internal improvement debt
      was finally paid in 1871.

123   80 Charles Bent (ed.), *History of Whiteside County* . . . , Morrison,
      Ill., 1877.

ACKNOWLEDGMENTS

This book, the first sustained study of the early Illinois capital and of Lincoln's primary adventures in elective office, owes its existence to many persons in addition to the author. Every historical writer incurs a great many obligations. The way was paved for the book by the members, directors, and officers of The Abraham Lincoln Association. Eight persons read the manuscript and made extremely valuable suggestions: George W. Bunn, Jr., Paul M. Angle, Benjamin P. Thomas, Roy P. Basler, and Mary E. Humphrey, officers of The Abraham Lincoln Association; Marion Dolores Bonzi, of the Association; Margaret A. Flint, of the Illinois State Historical Library; and Earl Schenck Miers, director of Rutgers University Press. Aid of a special sort was rendered by Dr. Harry E. Pratt, former Executive Secretary of the Association, who planned the book and began the research. Over a period of seven years Dr. Pratt assembled evidence and information which materially shortened the research task. To all these, as well as to libraries and other public institutions which helped, the author expresses his gratitude.

W. E. B;

137

INDEX